An Anthropologist in Japan

An *Anthropologist in Japan* is a highly personal narrative which provides unique insights into many elements of Japanese life. Hendry relates her experiences during a nine-month period of fieldwork in a Japanese seaside town. She sets out on a study of politeness but a variety of unpredictable events, including a volcanic eruption, a suicide and her son's involvement with the family of a powerful local gangster, begin to alter the direction of her research.

This volume exemplifies how much of anthropological knowledge is a product of chance, and how moments of insight can be embedded in a mass of everyday activity. The disturbing and disordered appear alongside the neat and the beautiful, and the vignettes here illuminate the education system, religious beliefs, politics, the family and the neighbourhood in modern Japan. An *Anthropologist in Japan* is reflexive anthropology in action. It demonstrates how ethnographic fieldwork can uniquely provide a deep understanding of linguistic and cultural difference.

An *Anthropologist in Japan* makes fascinating reading for anthropologists and for everyone interested in, or studying, Japanese society.

Joy Hendry is Professor of Social Anthropology at Oxford Brookes University. She has published numerous books and articles on Japan, including *Wrapping Culture* (1993), *Understanding Japanese Society* (Routledge, 1993) and *Interpreting Japanese Society* (ed.) (Routledge, 1998).

Association of Social Anthropologists
ASA Research Methods in Social Anthropology

Oral Traditions and the Verbal Arts
A guide to research practices
R. Finnegan

Applications in Computing for Social Anthropologists
M. Fischer

Reflexive Ethnography
A guide to researching selves and others
C. A. Davies

An Anthropologist in Japan

Glimpses of life in the field

Joy Hendry

London and New York

First published 1999 by Routledge
11 New Fetter Lane, London EC4P 4EE

Simultaneously published in the USA and Canada
by Routledge
29 West 35th Street, New York, NY 10001

© 1999 Joy Hendry

Typeset in Goudy by Routledge
Printed and bound in Great Britain by TJ International Ltd

British Library Cataloguing in Publication Data
A catalogue record for this book is available from the British
Library

Library of Congress Cataloguing in Publication Data
An Anthropologist in Japan: glimpses of life in the field/Joy
Hendry.
Includes bibliographical references and index.
1. Ethnology – Japan – Fieldwork. 2. Hendry, Joy. 3. Japan – social
life and customs. 4. Women ethnologists – Japan – Biography.
I. Title.
GN635. J2H45 1999
98 – 35095
306´.0952 – dc21
CIP

ISBN 0-415-19573-X (hbk)
ISBN 0-415-19574-8 (pbk)

Contents

Illustrations

Preface

The main body of this book is a personal, narrative account of a nine-month period spent investigating the subject of politeness in Japan. The work was mostly carried out in a seaside town, here depicted by a pseudonym, some two hours by train from Tokyo. Residence in this town, as a family with children attending the local school, brought us into contact with a fascinating cross-section of Japanese life. Documenting glimpses of this life is one aim of the book. The account follows some of the key events of the stay, more or less in chronological order, and it introduces the reader to a sample of local characters, slightly fictionalised in some cases to preserve the anonymity of the real people, but none the less lively and interesting for that.

The purpose of the project was an anthropological study, and the account is written to document the way in which knowledge is acquired during such an endeavour. The main method of research is participant observation, a practice where any part of daily life may be of professional interest, and the material has been selected to trace the way small pieces of information and possible interpretation gradually grew into an overarching framework of analysis. Much is learned by chance, picked up suddenly and without warning, and moments of insight are often embedded in a mass of everyday activity.

The long-term nature of anthropological study makes it possible to benefit from new ideas which occur unexpectedly like this, and even to rewrite the whole project if the circumstances demand it. It is not always easy to explain to grant-giving bodies, and colleagues in other disciplines, why anthropologists feel they can be rather vague about their initial aims when setting out for a period of fieldwork. This book not only documents a fairly radical change in purpose, but also aims to demonstrate the value of making that change. If the project had been too tightly delineated in the first place it might have been impossible to institute the kind of beneficial adjustments which took place, and the most interesting part of the result would have been lost.

Another advantage of participant observation is that the researcher comes to know groups of people rather well, and informal conversation with them allows for a check on the sorts of formal answers they may give to a questionnaire or one-off interview. There are often clear differences between what people say they do and what they actually do, and both differ again from what they say people ought to do. Given time, an anthropologist can identify all three levels, and these may be significant in themselves. The ideals people hold, even if they don't live by them, form an important element of any society, and people who consciously reject the ideals of their society may be amongst its most interesting members.

Moreover, finding out what people feel it is appropriate to say under certain circumstances, especially if this is different from their own individual behaviour, may reveal important information about modes of communication in that society. Any people may talk to a foreigner about things they have read about their own society, or they may modify what they say to accord with perceived ideas about the expectations of the foreigner. To take a specific example, Japanese educators are aware that aspects of their system have been criticised in the wider world, and they may talk at length to foreign researchers about government proposals for changing these elements, though they personally feel that the *status quo* is perfectly acceptable.

This could be described as diplomacy, or simply a polite way of respecting the ideas they expect the foreigner to hold, and short-term Western research on Japanese education is riddled with superficial niceties of this sort, which are then perpetuated as Japanese readers repeat them to new enquirers. This kind of 'respect' is itself an aspect of Japanese communication, which operates within the society too, and it is thus an important topic of study in its own right. In any society, people adapt their conversation depending on whom they are addressing, and what they say to an intimate friend will be different to the polite comments they may choose for a relative stranger. The study of the nature of these adjustments requires a considerable investment of time and care.

A further challenge for a researcher from a country like Britain, where politeness is already an important element of everyday life, is that he or she will expect to find the same sort of communication in another language. Learning words for 'please' and 'thank you' is often amongst the first things one seeks to do when travelling abroad, but the dictionary equivalents may have very different connotations in another society, and may be used at different times. In Japanese there are several words and phrases which correspond approximately to the English usage, and they each have further implications based on the relationship which exists between the people using them. Some other languages have no equivalent at all.

It is another important part of an anthropologist's work to delve beneath the dictionary definitions of words used in the language of the people they are studying, and their role beyond the strictly linguistic is to place that language in its appropriate social context. Indeed, social relations themselves form one of the main focuses of anthropological study, and the way these are expressed through language is one of the keys to understanding them. Native speakers tend to take a lot for granted in their everyday communication, and this is one reason why it is thought to be an advantage for anthropologists to be operating in a society which is not their own, as they must of necessity learn to stand outside their own expectations in discerning conventional usage.

Language is also important to anthropology because it is through language of one sort or another that people express their classification of the world around them. To gain an understanding of the thought processes of people who have grown up with another language, it is vital to work out how they classify the world in which they live, and the way they assign value to people and things in that world. When people from different backgrounds speak to one another in a common language, such as English, they may fail to communicate fully because each has a different idea of the meaning of the words he or she is using, sometimes even if both are native speakers. When both are using their own forms of politeness, the problems are compounded.

In Britain, Japanese visitors are said to be very polite, for example, but those Japanese visitors are not always happy with the treatment they receive. They may even be trying, politely, to communicate dissatisfaction, but they fail to make themselves clear, and the complaint is lost. People from other linguistic groups may make themselves too clear, and sound 'rude' in English, simply because they do not have the words in their own language to soften their tone. Those whose languages do not have an equivalent for 'please' to place at the end of a sentence are particularly vulnerable. On the other hand, a good understanding of such linguistic niceties is a powerful tool to effective and even manipulative use of language.

Help in overcoming misunderstanding between people from different backgrounds is an important element of what anthropologists can offer to the outside world once they have completed their studies; the subject matter of this book is not only about how such understanding is gained in the first place, but also about how deep the misunderstanding may be. The book therefore not only documents the way in which anthropologists work, it also identifies some of the specific forms of communication which are prevalent in Japan, and the way these may differ from the expectations of an English speaker. Since the general principles are much broader, the book could be of interest and value to anyone who operates seriously with people whose native tongue is radically different from their own.

As it turned out, this book and the study on which it is based go well beyond the use of spoken language, for it was gradually discerned that politeness in Japanese is communicated in all sorts of other ways. These modes of communication, which I came to call 'wrapping', are not confined to Japan, and it eventually became an interesting part of the work to seek parallels with other societies. The significance of 'wrapping' will become evident during the course of this book, but those who want to follow the ideas further should refer to the results of my study which were published in *Wrapping Culture: Politeness, Presentation and Power in Japan and Other Societies* (Oxford: Clarendon Press, 1993).

The original plan for this project made no mention of wrapping, however, for, in a way which probably reflected my prior understanding of politeness, I set out to make a study of 'speech levels'. More precisely, I was looking at a part of the Japanese language known as *keigo*, which incorporates very specific ways of expressing respect (a literal translation of *keigo* is indeed 'respect language'), but also of humbling oneself, and of generally raising the tone of a conversation. I was particularly interested in the way the use of this form of language expresses social distinctions and reflects social relationships, notably hierarchical ones, for textbook examples always seemed to couch their explanations in terms of hierarchical difference.

I had been inspired to take up the subject during a previous piece of fieldwork in Japan, when I had been focusing on the study of pre-school education, which seemed to impart the experience of hierarchical difference in a way which I thought would be interesting to follow up. I had also been advised by a very good friend that my student Japanese was sounding too informal, now that I was a university lecturer, and I had started studying *keigo* in my spare time. The two things came together, I thought, and I applied for a grant to return to Japan and make a detailed study of *keigo*, which would help me learn more about the hierarchical distinctions which seemed crucial to understanding social interaction in Japanese.

In preparing for the trip, I read general sociolinguistic theory about the use of politeness and 'speech levels' in different languages, and I gathered material already written about the specific case of Japanese. There is plenty written on *keigo* by Japanese authors, some of it serious linguistic and social analysis, some of it straightforward advice to native speakers who lack confidence in its use. Reading this abundant literature was a time-consuming task, for my Japanese reading speed is plodding, to say the least, but I was lucky enough to find a Japanese anthropologist, Yoko Hirose, studying in Oxford at the time, who not only agreed to help me to find and sift through the literature, but also became a part-time research assistant on her return to Japan.

This was a great help, because it became clear from this reading that the use of *keigo* is so embedded in the social relations of the people engaged in its use that a foreign researcher without a specific role in that society could well have an adverse influence on the language she heard. Yoko was taking up a position on her return which would involve much use of *keigo* and she agreed to act as a kind of 'mole', reporting back to me regularly on the observations she would make. She also continued to read and draw my attention to books and papers which appeared, and when my interest shifted to 'wrapping' she helped me to find works on that subject too. Although she is only mentioned occasionally in the text of this book, I owe her an enormous debt for sharing her time and ideas with me.

The reading and discussion we did in Oxford helped me to realise that I should try to find a location where I could fit into a community in my own right; as all the books reported on the greater use of *keigo* by women than men, it seemed that at least gender was on my side. A small pilot study amongst Japanese women of different social backgrounds living in Oxford helped to sharpen my initial focus as well as giving me a little extra confidence with my own use of this complicated linguistic system. Since I would be taking my children to Japan, I was encouraged by this first study to plan to supplement formal investigations with informal observations of language use amongst housewives and mothers I would meet through them.

In a nutshell, this is as far as the project had gone when the narrative opens, but it would be useful to make clear how this field trip fitted into my longer-term research in Japan, if only to clarify references in the text to previous visits. The research mentioned above on pre-school education had been carried out five years previously, in the same town, also with my children, so we had several friends and prior contacts, some of whom appear in this text too. This time, however, we lived in a new neighbourhood, which will be described in detail in Chapter 2, while Chapter 1 provides information about the first location and how my experience there influenced the choice of this new project.

Even this prior field trip was already my second major piece of participant observation. The first, on the subject of marriage, and the relative merits of 'love' and 'arranged' meetings, had been carried out in a completely different location, in a village in Kyushu, and we did return to that field site during the stay described here. Indeed, I made the visit a part of the study of *keigo*, and it was useful to encounter regional variation. There is reference in the text to this first visit, briefly in Chapter 6, but mostly in Chapter 18 and subsequently. I had stayed for a year on that occasion, so I came to know the villagers well. They were keen to see how my children were growing up, and some were game enough to answer questions yet again.

Finally, I had also spent several months living in Tokyo even before I took up the study of anthropology, and three of my friends from that visit appear in this book too. One is Takashi Tamaru, whose father's death is the subject of a part of Chapter 10, another is Kazuko Onishi, for whom I tried a bit of match-making in Chapter 17, and the third is Takako Shimagami, the heroine of this text, who twice introduced me to the area where we worked, and generously allowed me to share her family and social life on both occasions. Anthropologists can be quite a burden, so inquisitive are they about every minute detail of ordinary life, and it is difficult to find words enough to express the gratitude I owe to friends such as these, especially Takako, who also took care of many of our practical needs.

It will be clear from the text which follows how much debt an anthropologist builds up in his or her fieldwork, and this is a good opportunity to thank again all those who cooperated in the project. In general, Japan is an excellent place to do research, for people tend to respect academic inquiry, and respond with goodwill to all kinds of requests. Working with children in tow builds up another set of obligations, however, and I will for ever be grateful to the parents who helped me to negotiate the Japanese school system, to the teachers who put up cheerfully with two strange foreigners in their otherwise monocultural classrooms, and to my former student, Jenny Davidson, who came along to help out with domestic life, and certainly helped to keep us all sane.

Acknowledgement must also be made to the Economic and Social Research Council (United Kingdom) for the grant (reference no. G0023 2254/1) which funded this research, and to Professors Yoshida Teigo and Suzuki Takao who made it possible for me to be attached to the prestigious Keio University, to take advantage of its library and other facilities when I was in Tokyo, and to meet the now late Andrew Duff-Cooper, whose support is acknowledged in Chapter 13. They also invited me to give the seminar papers which are mentioned in the text. Finally, I would like to thank Annabel Black, Paul Collinson, Jenny Davidson, Takami Kuwayama, Glenda Roberts, Judy Skelton, Maren White, Jane Wilkinson and Teohna Williams for kindly reading drafts of the text, and making invaluable comments.

I trust that none of these people will object to the very personal nature of this book, which I would like to think will make a small contribution to a reflexive kind of anthropology, and those whose names I have changed will appreciate that I had their own interests in mind. As mentioned above, a researcher, especially a foreigner, can hardly fail to influence a project about a subject as socially embedded as politeness. Indeed, any anthropological investigation involves so much of the personality and background of the researcher that it has become an issue of some concern in the field. Perhaps paradoxically, then, this book seeks to demonstrate, precisely through a detailed examination of the personal life of the researcher, the unique value of the methods of anthropology for deep and serious understanding of general linguistic and cultural difference.

I hope that the book will also provide interesting and revealing glimpses of Japanese life. It will soon be clear that no attempt has been made to paper over the cracks. The disturbing and disordered have been included along with the neat and beautiful. The vignettes presented are necessarily cursory and truncated, but they include aspects of the education system, of religious beliefs, of politics, albeit mostly the underside, and of the family and neighbourhood in modern Japan.

Finally, I hope that the book may make a contribution to the wider aim that I believe is made especially possible by the subject of social anthropology, namely to help overcome the dreadful propensity of people to misunderstand one another.

JH

Oxford, 1998

Part I

Settling in and making contacts

Chapter 1

Arrival...and an invitation

The development of the research idea explained, some needs of fieldwork outlined, and first steps taken to set up the project.

Toyama lies almost at the tip of the Boso Peninsula, a few degrees inside sub-tropical latitudes. This factor allows its inhabitants to cultivate fields of flowers while much of the rest of Japan is still waiting for the winter to pass. Tennis and golf are played here throughout the year, and in the summer long sandy beaches rarely fill with the hordes of bathers found nearer to the urban sprawl. The sea is cleaner, too, and the surrounding hills provide a cool retreat when the heat becomes excessive. A string of villages spread away on either coast, home to fishing families who help keep the nation's culinary demands supplied, and inland, beyond the developed area of golf-courses and other sports complexes, farmers grow carnations and keep cattle. Rice and vegetables are grown too, for this is a green and abundant piece of land.

As I sat on the air-conditioned express train, approaching Toyama at the end of the long journey from my home in England, I began to experience a feeling of exquisite anticipation. Initial plans had been made, leave from normal routines had been secured, and funds for the next nine months were safely in the bank. During the course of the flight from London the anxiety of the last frenzied weeks of preparation and desk-clearing had gradually lifted, and I had been able to turn my undivided attention to thoughts of the time ahead. Life during fieldwork is ostensibly in one's own hands, to arrange in the way which seems most appropriate to the research. On the other hand, anything might happen. An anthropologist is his or her own chief research tool, and any or all of the encounters which arise 'in the field' might contribute to the final result.

The July sunshine, an hour before an infernal source of heat impeding and irritating the transfer of my luggage from one station platform to another, began to glint appealingly through the abundant foliage which grows between the railway line and the sea. This part of Japan is separated from the super-populated central plain, where Tokyo lies, by a range of mountains which runs right down to the coast. As the train makes its way through the tunnels, built to provide a link, the developed part of the scenery gives way by degrees to a more relaxing, rural aspect, a gentle contrast with the dense, hurried environment which pervades the north of the prefecture.

Some five years before, I had spent six months living in Toyama, in a fishing community a few miles from the centre of the city. The south-bound train passes through the local station, and I was able to look out of the window and see the tiny house we had called home during that time. It was a white splash lodged between the fields of ripening rice and the darker green hills which lay behind. My children had been small. Callum had learned to walk there; Hamish had run down the road each day to play with his friends at White Lily Kindergarten. Our nanny had fallen for a local boy. She had also fallen off her bicycle into a rice field after having too much sake at the station bar.

This incident had brought about an interesting development in our relationship with the headmistress of the kindergarten in whose house we had lived and who helped in many ways with the research I had been doing on pre-school education. It was just one in a series of impromptu events which add leaps and bounds to the sum of knowledge gained during fieldwork. Such insights contrast sharply with the small, rather predictable steps made in the planned progress of research, and sometimes spark off a whole new line of thinking. In fact it was this headmistress, Mrs Takahashi, or Mrs T, as we came to call her, who had provided direct inspiration for the new project on which I was about to embark.

She was a well-dressed woman, with an extraordinary presence, and she spoke, almost always, in formal and extremely polite language. She seemed to choose her words carefully, insinuating meaning far beyond a simple translation of the phrases, and I had often felt in a situation of competition when conversing with her. She had a way of putting people on their best behaviour, of keeping them in order, and she also seemed somehow to inspire most of her associates to work extremely hard – for her and her kindergarten, or on its behalf, though certainly not always without private complaint.

It was the language which had interested me at first. I had been attempting to notch up my own Japanese during that stay, using a book on the subject of *keigo*, which covers polite, respectful and formal language. However, while it helped me to get the phrases right, it failed to explain the range of possibilities which appropriate language could open up for influence and self-presentation. Officially, *keigo* is a way to express relative hierarchy; in practice it seemed to be much more, and this is what I hoped to investigate in the new study I was about to start. What exactly were Japanese people doing with these niceties of expression, layers of politeness and subtleties of meaning?

My previous research had involved much time spent with mothers and their young children, and I had learned that it is important to acquire these different levels of politeness as early as possible. Mothers took trouble that the tiniest of children should hear only the most exemplary language, and they would carefully repeat phrases appropriate for particular situations, sometimes even if there was no adult present to hear them. I had been told that those who learn later never quite achieve the same convincing facility with the use of these special polite forms, and since Japanese, like their British counterparts, judge one another by their manners of speech, this seemed also to be an important way to pass on social allegiances.

So here I was. I had received a grant from the British government, and I had arranged to spend nine months looking at this Japanese politeness phenomenon. Prior reading had made clear that there is considerable variation in the use of polite language, both regionally and socially, so I planned to spend a few weeks travelling around a little and discussing my project with Japanese friends and scholars. Since my children, now aged 6 and 9, were shortly to join me again, I also needed to find a school for them, and arrange accommodation. Toyama was my first port of call.

An old friend, Takako, whom I had met on my very first visit to Japan some fifteen years earlier, now lived in Toyama, and she had been a pillar of support the previous time. She had found and introduced me to Mrs Takahashi, explained the various local facilities for mothers with babies and small children, and turned up regularly with enticing invitations to escape from the occasionally rather claustrophobic atmosphere of the house and kindergarten which became my major work-place. Her children were even younger than mine at the time, so we had shared a common interest in the subject of study, and we had often discussed details of the work in more relaxed surroundings.

In the interim, Takako had brought her children to England, and together we had pondered the best way to put the new project into practice. The study of politeness could be quite slippery, since declaring an interest might make people self-conscious, shrouding their normal behaviour with a front of unusual *politesse*, or impoliteness. Should I therefore invent another subject of study so that I could listen to people's language without their knowledge? It hardly seemed ethical. I would certainly need to get to know people so well that they could relax in my company. I would also need to see the same people in several different situations so that I could observe the way their language changed.

All this is of course quite possible using participant observation, but I would need to establish relations with an existing group of people who know one another well – a village, a neighbourhood or a work group, perhaps – so that time could be spent with the same people in different activities. I could then not only talk to individual people and ask them questions, I could also listen to them talking amongst themselves. I could have them explain not only their own behaviour, but also that of others around them. So I needed to find such a group – not just a home, and a school, but some kind of a group to attach myself to, to spend time with, to live amongst.

In the case of this new research, it also seemed a good idea to try to join several groups, so that I could observe the variation in politeness amongst different types of people. The language of White Lily private kindergarten contrasted sharply with the local dialect of the fishing families who lived around it, for example, but I wasn't sure how representative of Japan Toyama would be. Hence the decision to travel first. Yoko, the research assistant I had recruited in Oxford, would be in Tokyo, only two hours away, but I had been offered reduced rates for the children at the English school in Kobe, several hours beyond that. I planned to make a temporary base amongst friends while I looked into the various possibilities.

As the train pulled into the station, Takako stood on the platform, smiling broadly, a small daughter clutched in either hand. We had barely exchanged pleasantries when she issued me with an invitation, one which offered an instant solution to several of my requirements. It was her daughter's birthday the next day, she explained, and her friends would come round accompanied by their mothers. The group formed the hard core of a collection of young housewives whom Takako met regularly. She was close to these women, so she felt we should come clean about my intentions, but she also saw no reason why I should not become a member of the group myself. They engaged in a number of activities, some associated with the kindergarten attended by their children, which happened to be my old place of research, but others purely recreational. I could certainly join their tennis class, Takako thought, and we'd think of plenty more opportunities to meet.

Furthermore, one of these women was about to vacate a house, which belonged, like Takako's, to the hospital where their two husbands worked as doctors. Takako suggested we ask her about it. If it was suitable, the hospital might be prepared to rent it out to me for a few months. Another of the women in the group was married to a member of the family which owned the hospital. He worked in the office, where he had great influence, and Takako felt sure we could arrange something through him.

As if this wasn't enough, Takako had even been down to the local Education Office to enquire about schools. The response had been quite encouraging, for my boys had been offered places, but not in the local school attended by all the other children in the neighbourhood. Since they knew little Japanese, it had been suggested that they attend a more central school where there was apparently a special class they could enter. This school was also the showpiece of the town, with the latest facilities, so it would be worth having a look, she thought. Again, one of the mothers coming to the party could help, for her son was already enrolled there.

What a welcome! After twenty-two hours of travel, with a nine-hour time-change, I was feeling slightly jaded, but this was all excellent news. Takako had found an existing set of people for me to join. Her group of friends (or *nakama*) could become one I would get to know well too, with no need to invent excuses to meet, and I could see them in a variety of situations. Though they would know of my interest – and, indeed, at least one was most self-conscious about her language at the party – hopefully, they would see me so often they would forget to behave in an extraordinary way.

Takako was certainly doing her best to help out again. The party was not until the next day, and although I felt so sleepy during the course of it that I had to slip away, I was able to meet everyone, and broach all the appropriate subjects. We ate bowls of fresh fruit with a wonderful cake, and drank coffee spiced with Bailey's. I found out about houses and schools, and set up more initial contacts in a couple of hours than I might have hoped to make in a good week's work. Takako's friends seemed equally enthusiastic to join in with the project, and I went off to doze feeling most positive.

During the following few weeks I did travel around, making a preliminary survey of differences in polite language in various parts of Japan. I also looked at other possibilities for the long-term study, but I found nothing as appealing as Takako and her Toyama *nakama*. I visited the English school in Kobe, and I was even shown some of the strange hybrid accommodation an associate of the head thought might appeal to a foreigner, but when I found my children would be especially welcome because they desperately needed native speakers, I decided that we might as well stick with a Japanese school. As the start of the school term began to approach, then, I returned to Toyama and moved into our hospital house.

Chapter 2

The neighbourhood
A 'world of blossom and willow'

Establishing good relations with members of the immediate neighbourhood, getting to know its inhabitants, and making some
discoveries about its history.

The house we were to live in was adequate for our needs, and once we
were inside, with the doors and windows shut, it was quite charming. It
had a small entrance hall, with a cupboard for the shoes in the usual
Japanese style, and a surface on top which later became the showplace
for the creations I brought home from my flower-arranging class. To
the left, there was a well-equipped kitchen, with a table and enough
chairs to accommodate us all for family meals, although the fit was a
little tight for the less trim Western body. To the right was the bath-
room and loo, and one Western-style room, with its own hinged door.
Through beyond the kitchen were two rooms joined by a set of sliding
doors, with springy *tatami* matting on the floor, and spacious cupboards
along the whole of one wall.

This last arrangement is appropriate for the traditional Japanese
lifestyle. During the day, one sits, works and plays around a large, low
table, close to the fresh, reedy aroma of the distinctive *tatami* mats,
which can be smartened up with cushions for entertaining. In the
evening, the table is raised, and mattresses and covers are brought out
from the cupboards, to be laid down for sleeping. I decided to put the
children in the inner room, so that their door could be slid shut in the
evenings. The Western room I set aside for Jenny, an ex-student who
had gamely agreed to come and share the experience. I made my own
sleeping area in the middle room, which during the day was a sort of
helm of operations, also containing the cooling/heating machine and
the television. Fortunately, for most of the time we were there, I also

had a room where I could work, on the second floor of Takako's house next door.

Most of the windows ran along the back of the house, a row of sliding glass doors, which could be further secured by pulling across the metal storm shutters. There was a narrow path beyond this, enclosed by a thick hedge, which cut out the view of, but not the sounds from, a neighbour with a loud, petulant voice which easily out-ranked in decibels those of her two small, rather pathetic-sounding children. In the summer, this was irritating, though I was slightly comforted to know that she was usually so wrapped up in keeping order in her own home that our noisier children would probably go unnoticed. In the winter, when we carefully sealed out the cold, she could hardly be heard.

Outside the front door, the view was very different from our last Japanese house. Immediately we had to make a sharp turn to avoid walking into the rusting iron stairway which led to the upper apartment of this hospital house. We then found ourselves in a rough gravelled area which served as a space for the neighbour's car, our four bicycles, and all manner of children's games. To the left was Takako's house, with a slightly domesticated space at the back acting as home to a swing and a children's table and chairs, though it didn't quite qualify to be called a garden. To the right, separated a little by some foliage, and a dip into an area which had been cared for on a longer-term basis, lived the Tanaka family.

On its fourth aspect the compound bridged the deepish brook running parallel to the narrow approach road which closed off the square. Little more than an asphalted path, though big enough to allow a motor vehicle through, this thoroughfare led out to a busy main road, some fifty yards to the right. To the left it provided access to more houses and, as I was later to discover, a quiet and quite fascinating path through to the children's school. Another couple of houses stood opposite, set back from the road, and one of these had a carefully cultivated garden in front sporting an abundance of bonsai trees.

It is customary in Japan to take a small gift to the neighbours when one moves into a new house. It is also usual to contribute to a monthly collection for immediate local expenses, to expect to be asked to cooperate with the cleaning of paths and streams, and for a notice-board to circulate at regular intervals with news of local interest. I knew all this from previous experience, and I decided enquiries about this sort of activity would not only be prudent for future relations with people I might meet, but also perhaps make possible another group for the purposes of my research.

I thus approached Takako. She was not entirely encouraging. She did tell me the names and occupations of a few of the neighbours, including information about those with children, although it was only one of the two houses opposite which had any approximately the same ages as ours, and these were girls. She also outlined the duties expected, which included turning out on a Sunday morning once a month to clean the brook – which she referred to as a ditch.

She had herself been responsible for collecting the neighbourhood dues in a previous year, but she complained that some of the people in the group were either too mean or too poor to pay so she had ended up having to subsidise them. The system actually made provision for such recalcitrants, by taking on their debt as a group, but the sums were so small that Takako thought her own solution less troublesome. The monthly sub was the yen equivalent of between one and two pounds sterling, slightly variable according to circumstances. Evidently not everyone in Japan is as wealthy as one might have been led to expect.

Initially, then, I made a fairly formal visit to the current administrator of our immediate neighbourhood group, who assured me I could live there on a temporary basis without making this expensive contribution. I insisted, however, explaining that I wanted to become a proper neighbour, and I would also like to receive the circulating notice-board. He agreed, though his dismissive remarks about some Koreans who had formerly lived nearby made me hope that we would be classified differently in his assignment of value to humans who had the misfortune not to be born Japanese. 'What were they like?' I had asked about the Koreans. 'Well, they were Koreans,' he had answered. That was apparently enough.

I also asked him to explain the wider administrative system, and to give me the names and addresses of the characters, political and bureaucratic, who saw to the day-to-day running of life in this part of the city. I asked him, too, about events which affected us on a geographical basis. Eventually I planned to spread my net wider than the immediate neighbours, and I wanted also to try to characterise our location in the make-up of the city. He was a little reticent on this last question, and, indeed, about the inhabitants of our own larger district, but he told me of an area sports-day which was soon to be held, which did prove useful for meeting more people, and explained that I had missed the annual festival.

Actually, I had not missed the annual festival entirely, for the evening air had been full of the strains of drums and flutes when I stayed with Takako in July. This had been the children practising, she explained, for during the day itself, huge floats are pulled around different sections of the neighbourhood, carrying young musicians, who take it in turns to provide the incessant accompanying music. Money is also collected from the houses as a float lurches by, but to their shame, the administrator admitted, the residents of our particular section were so uncharitable that no one had organised for a float to come round our way. That shocked me, for though few people will assign any religious meaning to these local festivals, most are willing enough to take part.

It seemed that there was something strange about this little neighbourhood, indeed about the wider district. I was definitely not being told all. Takako had only been there for a shortish time herself. She had previously lived in a much more friendly part of town where her neighbours had not only been charming and welcoming to the incoming doctor's family, they had also made her a part of their lives. She was therefore rather scathing about this new location. She had decided not to bother to try to integrate further since her family was likely soon to move away. My own previous experiences had also been much more positive, but I would not give up so easily. I decided to make some further visits.

My immediate neighbours on the other side seemed nice enough. Mrs Tanaka was a middle-aged woman with two grown sons, who came around with some of their old toys when she heard I had two younger boys who were shortly to arrive. I saw her regularly, for hers was the next house on the list for the circulating notice-board, and the rule was that this should be passed from hand to hand. She lived with her husband, whose younger brother turned out to be a teacher at the boys' school, and her husband's mother. The family had apparently been there for longer than anyone else in the immediate vicinity, and the grandmother was also said to be the oldest person in the neighbourhood. I decided to make a special visit.

Mrs Tanaka senior was bed-ridden, but she was by no means unwilling to talk. Indeed, she seemed to welcome the opportunity to have company for a morning. Her bed was in a back room, facing a window which overlooked a long, rather pretty garden, and she sat propped up with pillows, chattering away at speed. She was very old and quite wizened, full of self-pity about her difficult life and current condition, but she was also happy to reminisce about the way things used to be. She went so fast, and in such a rambling fashion, that I had trouble keeping up, but some of her tales were intriguing.

The house we sat in was indeed one of the oldest in the neighbourhood, she recounted, but everything had changed completely since her youth. This was an area where people would come to have fun, she sighed, and she herself had been one of the major attractions. Her nickname had been Osato – a possible translation of this is 'Sugary', or perhaps 'Honey' – and life had been so good. The house itself had been a restaurant, serving traditional Japanese food, but there had been all kinds of other entertainment, it seems, here and in most of the houses around. She tried to give me a more detailed description of the activities which went on, including the use of a neighbouring building comprising two storeys of very small apartments, but some of the vocabulary was perhaps mercifully lost on my innocent ears. In a typically Japanese fashion, we became involved in the analysis of a charming euphemism about a world of flowers and trees, willow trees to be precise. Later, at home with the dictionary, the meaning was clarified. She had been describing the 'world of blossom and willow', quite simply a 'red-light district'. So this was the history of the area I had picked out for my children. Thank goodness the Council had taken over the building in question to house people on welfare.

During the Second World War, there had been a shortage of rice, with a consequent lack of sake, so the Tanakas' business had collapsed. Since that time, many people had moved in and out of the neighbourhood, and there had been some reconstruction. The sites of the hospital houses, occupied by Takako's family and ourselves, had also been bars in the olden days, Mrs Tanaka senior recounted wistfully. The only place left retaining any of the old atmosphere was the 'eel shop', a specialist restaurant out on the main road. Here they still knew a thing or two about looking after the customers, she said, and I resolved to make a visit there too.

Mrs Tanaka senior was otherwise rather dismissive about her neighbours. The Koreans, who had reputedly been in the *pachinko* pin-ball parlour business, had been *kawatta*, 'different' or 'odd', so she had hardly spoken to them. A little farther out, but part of the same women's group, were some farming people, but all they wanted to talk about was the success or otherwise of the rice harvest, so she had pulled out of that organisation. Women in general were far too full of gossip, she felt, always concerned about who's doing this and who's doing that. She used an expression for 'outsiders' to refer to a wide range of people, and my overall impression of this old lady was that the life she had known and loved had shattered many years ago, perhaps with her youth, as well as with the war.

My visit to the 'eel shop' a few days later clarified the situation quite a lot. This was now a most respectable establishment, which I had already noticed on the corner of our access road for its distinctive exterior. Built in the style of a nineteenth-century town-house, smartly maintained with fresh white paint and an attractively shaped gabled roof, it stood out from an otherwise uninteresting row of modern buildings. A tasteful sign stood in front displaying the name in a flourishing hand, which appeared again on the cloth curtains that hung during the day in front of the sliding entrance door. Inside, too, the décor was attractive, though in a subdued, entirely unostentatious way.

The daughter-in-law of the family which ran the 'eel shop' was among Takako's acquaintances, for their grandchild attended White Lily Kindergarten, and the mothers stood together daily waiting for its bus to pick up their children. Sometimes she came to the compound between our houses to push her younger child on the swing behind Takako's house, and she had called me over to the back of the restaurant one morning to see the bucket of wriggling eels one of the employees was washing out. She was sure her father-in-law would be pleased to talk to me. He knew the area well, and he had a huge circle of acquaintances.

The 'eel shop' turned out to be among the best-known restaurants in town. Mr Izuki was indeed a willing informant, and secured our further business by inviting me, for our talk, into one of the private dining rooms which we later hired to celebrate special occasions and entertain important visitors. It was an upstairs room, with a view over the houses to a white castle on an intriguingly none-too-distant hill. A slight breeze blew through the mosquito netting, moving the warm summer air and emphasising the aromatic atmosphere, a combination of the cedar room-posts and the fresh *tatami* matting.

Although Izuki-*san* had himself bought and developed the 'eel shop' some years later, he confirmed that the area where we lived had previously been a red-light district, a place for entertainment within easy reach of the big hospital across the road. It had survived the war, though with a considerable drop in quality, only to be virtually snuffed out in the early fifties when the system of licensed prostitution was stopped. Many of the people who had owned or worked in the establishments in question were still living in or near their original houses, but they sought their livelihood elsewhere. It was possible, I supposed, that some of them had turned to illegal ways of making a living, if the law had suddenly put them out of business. This would perhaps explain the feeling I had that there was something still to know.

I visited Izuki-*san* again later to discuss *keigo*, and the importance of care for the customer. He talked about the way an initial polite approach to strangers must gradually be dropped as the same people return, so that they feel welcome and cared for in a more intimate way. He was evidently skilled in this because comments about the restaurant usually complimented the good company as well as the décor and the excellence of the eels. Mr Izuki talked of other details of the neighbourhood too, but if he gave any hints about the extent of the illegality I would eventually unearth there, I certainly failed to pick them up at that first meeting.

Chapter 3

The hospital...and a strange encounter

Further good contacts set up, some progress made with the language research, and an opportunity arises to learn from an unexpected situation.

A few steps from our neighbourhood, just across the main road into town, stood the Toyama Hospital, where Takako's husband was employed as a psychiatrist. It was a general hospital, with several specialist departments other than psychiatry, and the buildings formed a landmark familiar even to people who took their patronage elsewhere. Despite its name, the hospital was privately owned, and in a small garden to one side of the main entrance stood busts of the three men who had taken a turn at being in charge of it. In the usual Japanese fashion, these men were medical directors, members of a family dynasty, and since medicine is perhaps the most highly ranked profession in Japan, they had also been veritable pillars of the town's elite.

Partly to offset the evident lack of community spirit within the neighbourhood, and partly to take an interest in the benefactors who were allowing us the use of a house, I decided to investigate the world of hospital life a little. I knew that, as elsewhere, there would be a fairly clear system of hierarchy amongst the hospital employees, and I thought it might be interesting to see how this was manifested in language. I was also interested to see how sickness and the consequent dependence on relative strangers would influence the social position of an individual, and, conversely, whether social position and economic advantage would make a difference to the care available in this world of health care as a private enterprise.

There were also some immediate connections, of course, and these could be followed up without delay. I had already become acquainted with the hospital office where I had arranged to appear monthly, with my rent, and my contact person there was Mr Kawana, the husband of one of the *nakama* from the initial children's party. He also happened to be heir to a large family home as the non-medical son of the third head of the hospital, and he had thus been engaged in the enterprise in an administrative capacity. He was happy to introduce me to his cousins, the Hosakas, who comprised the current hospital head, his flamboyant wife, and a younger brother who ran a Rehabilitation Centre next door.

This was a good contrast to the local neighbourhood, for though these families lived only over the road, they represented the height of respectability in Toyama. In fact, they were themselves almost as much Tokyo people as Toyama people, for Mr Hosaka senior had married into the Kawana line when the founder of the hospital was left without a medical heir, and he had continued to maintain a residence at his family home in the city. After the initial years of elementary education, his sons had been sent to a private school in Tokyo, where it was thought they would receive better preparation for the difficult entry to medical school. This experience also ensured a certain polishing of their manners, for it was clear that a close association with Tokyo definitely represented sophistication in Toyama.

The usual system of passing a family business from father to son is subject to any number of compromises in the interests of keeping efficient continuity in the family, and the senior Mr Hosaka, second hospital director as son-in-law of the first, had been succeeded initially by Mr Kawana's father, a nephew of the founder. His own son had thus established something of a reputation in Tokyo before he was called upon to take his place as the next heir, and he now ran the Toyama Hospital for three or four days of the week and continued to see his city patients on Mondays. This arrangement suited his wife, too, for she was involved in practising and giving classes in a traditional form of Japanese dance – again mostly in Tokyo.

The younger Hosaka brother, on the other hand, had gone into broadcasting, and he had spent years working as a television announcer for NHK before deciding to retire to the family's provincial home where he set up and ran the Rehabilitation Centre as a business. He had shocked the local community at an early age by marrying a maid who came to work in his brother's house, but he had evidently been accepted back into the inner circle of Toyama dignitaries for he later invited me to join him at a harvest festival ceremony at a big local shrine when he was called upon to represent just such a group.

This Mr Hosaka (Rehabili – to distinguish him from the other) actually turned out to be a splendid informant, perhaps because his experience as a TV announcer had made him particularly aware of some of the intricacies of language use. He had also been acutely aware of having to adjust his own forms of speech as he straddled the various social groups represented by his parents, who insisted he develop a facility with the politest of language, his primary-school friends, who scorned anything but the crudest of local dialect, and his adolescent Tokyo associates; moreover, undoubtedly, though he didn't mention this, he had to find a way of getting on with his in-laws.

He gave me a lot of information about the stringent requirements of broadcasting, and how these had changed over the years. He also explained the various different forms of speech expected on the television screen, for in Japan news is transmitted in a very impersonal, formal type of language quite distinct from that used to present more chatty programmes. The latter generally require two presenters, one to do the talking and the other to make appropriate responses, for it is virtually impossible to speak anything but the most formal Japanese without identifying the relative social level of the audience. Since the viewers would obviously represent a huge range of total strangers, a category requiring too polite a level of discourse, employing a respondent is a neat ploy to allow a more intimate and friendly style.

Hosaka-san (Rehabili) was also quite willing to discuss something that others, especially women, seemed to be more reticent about, namely the way people assess one another based on the levels of *keigo* they were able to command. There would seem to be no question that people do make very clear judgements about each other in this way, just as the British do, for it is even said that it takes three generations to be at ease with all the intricacies of higher-class polite behaviour, however much money you might acquire in your own lifetime. Equally, it is almost impossible convincingly to adopt a local dialect within a short space of time. It seems that openly making such judgements about people is not really very acceptable, however.

Mr Hosaka also pointed something out to me in passing that later took on much more significance in my research, namely that language is not the only indicator of such social differences. He mentioned dress sense, and this I had to concede was a mark of social differentiation elsewhere too, though the recognition of subtle hints of background could be harder to identify for an outsider than forms of speech. What would take longer for me to grasp, however, was the enormous range of other indications of culture, upbringing, education and degrees of refinement in a Japanese view.

Mrs Hosaka (Hosp.) was a good example of a problem for me in this respect. Her language was, as far as I could tell, extremely polite, and she seemed to exhibit other signs of a well-dressed, well-brought-up woman. After all, she was married to the director of a hospital, and she practised an extremely refined form of traditional Japanese dance. However, when members of the *nakama* discussed her manner, they were able to identify further details of her background and general character which made clear immediately that I had still a lot to learn. Mrs H was from Shitamachi, for example, an older part of 'lower' Tokyo which was to be distinguished from Yamanote, literally 'upper mountain', which also stood for a more refined social category.

Mrs Hosaka herself explained some of the differences between these two categories and the way they sound in contrast to each other. She said the more refined version of *keigo* is terribly 'slow' and sometimes quite irritating to those who were brought up to operate more speedily. I had heard the same distinction expressed between the language of full-time 'professional' housewives, who have the time and leisure to care for all the subtle niceties of polite behaviour, and the faster language of women who also go out to work. Though I was without doubt a member of the second category myself, I was fascinated by these characteristics of Japanese refinement and I stiffened my resolve to learn from my new group of housewives some of the secrets of their art.

Mrs Hosaka also explained an important point to me about the use of *keigo* in Toyama. The local people here don't use many of the more refined words, she noted, so it would be rude to make them feel uncomfortable by replying to their local language in terms more appropriate for Tokyo. Indeed, it would be a direct contradiction of the point of polite language, which is surely to avoid such rudeness. Her husband found it much more conducive to good relations with his patients to drop a few expressions from the local dialect into his speech, she added. They knew he was doing this for their benefit, since his normal language was the standard form, and they were delighted.

Some of my other Toyama acquaintances who had moved in from outside never seemed to learn this simple principle. They continued to use the language they had found appropriate elsewhere, and they were simply regarded as cold or even stuck-up by their new neighbours. Over the next few months, I would have plenty of opportunity to observe, analyse and discuss women's language with them, and I learned a lot by asking people to describe the way they felt about the language used by others. For me, it took time to develop a feeling for subtleties in the use of *keigo*, but an incident which took place not long after I had settled in was perhaps an early opportunity to begin to develop this facility.

It was around eleven o'clock one morning. I was returning home from a couple of visits, and just about to round the corner of our street, when I heard a voice call out 'Hi' in a most compelling manner. It was unusual to be addressed in English, but a fair foreigner such as myself stands out a mile in a Japanese neighbourhood and this fact in itself was not unusual. The speaker approached enthusiastically across the road, however, following her initial greeting with a fairly detailed speech of self-presentation, still in English. She was the daughter of a lawyer, Mr B, who, she explained, was a well-known man in the town, and she had recently visited the United States.

She was a youngish Japanese woman, smiling and cheerful, and she was dressed in a colourful, expensive-looking dress. She spoke as if we had already met, and I was not entirely certain that I had not perhaps encountered her briefly during my previous visit, but I certainly had no recollection of it. In fact, she made me feel a little invaded, and I walked on towards my house in the hope of shaking her off. She clung fiercely to my side, however, pressing her conversation on me and asking questions about my presence here. I answered them as politely as I could, unwilling to upset anyone who might live locally, but I was entirely unprepared for the way she followed me into the house. She certainly lacked some of the usual Japanese reticence I had come to expect.

Since she seemed to have forced a visit upon me, and she was anyway disturbingly unfamiliar in her approach, I remembered how often one learns from an unusual situation, and offered her some juice. She continued to chatter away, though she soon abandoned her English, and we talked comparatively of the education and legal systems in Japan, the US and Britain. The woman was undoubtedly quite well informed, but she was excessively defensive on behalf of Japan, whose arrangements she argued vehemently were infinitely superior in every respect. She herself claimed to be extremely clever and to have no fewer than three university degrees. She took every opportunity to emphasise her good points, and those of her family, as well as singing the praises of her country.

At one point, quite suddenly, she remembered to apologise for having barged so rudely into my house, and became very upset when I reassured her that our conversation was interesting to me because I was here to do research. Most of my Japanese associates found being involved in such activity quite flattering, but she was aghast. 'You mean I'm raw material?' she hissed. I agreed, but then quickly changed my tune as her reaction was so fierce. She proceeded to accuse me of 'running away', or back-tracking, which of course I was. I continued to do so, in words as firm and sincere as I could muster....

What happened next was instinctive rather than a conscious decision, for I found myself resorting to a series of fixed polite expressions which are used when entertaining has come to an end: 'I'm sorry I haven't been able to offer you anything worthwhile,' 'Do, please, come and visit again.' Her response was immediate. She replied in exactly the same tones, with the phrases which are conventionally used in reply. She thanked me for my hospitality, my time and my interest, set off for the doorway, slipped into her shoes, and was gone.

What a strange encounter! I felt quite exhausted by it and began to wonder whether my visitor had been a stray patient from the psychiatric department of Takako's husband, Minoru. Actually, something about our last series of formulaic exchanges had reminded me of the way Japanese people sometimes speak to me. It struck me that these stereotypical greetings are rather useful in a situation of social insecurity. I had felt unsure how to behave, though I had thought myself rather well versed in normal Japanese social interaction. Suddenly I understood how some Japanese people become quite disorientated by the unusual situation of a foreigner speaking Japanese.

My visitor had certainly been lacking in some of the social graces more usually encountered in Japan. I began to carry the comparison further. She had been 'strange', and a character for 'strange' in Japanese is used to describe foreigners who fail to conform to stereotypes. If they speak a foreign language and fumble with chopsticks, they are simply foreigners. If they try to do things in a Japanese way, particularly by becoming at ease with the language, and chopsticks, they are most decidedly 'strange'! The same character, incidentally, which also more neutrally means 'different', is also used in a slang expression to describe the mentally ill. I got up from my seat and went round to Takako's house.

It turned out that the woman who had called was indeed a patient from the psychiatric department. She was an out-patient, and Minoru later gave her strict instructions not to bother me again. I was relieved, though also slightly disappointed, but I did not wish to interfere with his judgement as her doctor. He was less enthusiastic than me about my comparison between foreigners and the mentally ill in a Japanese view, but he conceded that each could cause anxiety in social intercourse. He elaborated a little about the way people assess one another when they meet in a kind of informal power struggle – an effort to place each other in a system of relative hierarchy – but foreigners and the mentally ill don't even agree about the rules, he explained.

It was a difficult conversation, because he was convinced of a physiological basis for psychiatric disorder, but I found it rather disturbing. There are certainly cultural differences in diagnoses of mental illness, and we pursued for some time a discussion about eccentricity. Minoru mentioned a Japanese expression that 'a single sheet of paper lies between genius and stupidity', but he also explained that nurses don't like working in the psychiatric department because his patients are 'rude'. They use inappropriate language, and give gifts at inappropriate times. I had actually witnessed this when he had shown me round his wards and one of his charges had kept pressing small items of her belongings on me. This is a world where gifts can be powerful, if presented in the right way.

The incident helped me to decide very quickly about the school with a 'special class' which I had been offered for my children. Further enquiry elicited the information that it was a class for the mentally handicapped. The mentally handicapped, like foreign children, have trouble with their language, so this had apparently seemed suitable. They would all get extra help. I began to understand the logic behind the suggestion, but I was appalled at the idea. Perhaps this was my own prejudice, but I set off the next morning, without further ado, to visit the more local school.

Chapter 4

The school...and a fight

Setting up practical arrangements for the family has its problems, reveals some vulnerability in the researcher, but opens up some new avenues for the research.

The walk to Toyama Primary School was almost enough in itself to convince me that this would be a better arrangement for my children, for pupils are expected to travel on foot and the path was enchanting. A left turn out of the compound led through a few of our neighbourhood houses, over a quiet road, and into a footpath which ran between a picturesque graveyard and another row of houses and gardens. It passed a small playground on the left, which provided a nearby play area, and a shady buffer zone between this residential district and the rice fields beyond. A little farther on, the path ran right out into a larger park which had evidently been recently developed.

This was the ancient site of the residence of a local lord by the name of Satomi, apparently, and the castle I had seen from the 'eel shop' was a reconstruction of his seat of power. Steps led invitingly away through the trees to the top of the hill where the castle was situated, but the path to school was straight on. It passed next through the grounds of a large shrine, only skirting the back of the main buildings, but a glance to the right revealed several interesting smaller shrines, each marked with a wooden archway, and each with offerings placed before it, presumably to the deity represented. After that, one passed the modern buildings of the municipal museum, along the side of a cultivated field, past a few more houses, and, quite abruptly, arrived at the school gate.

Like other Japanese primary schools, the buildings were functional rather than attractive, ranged in front of a large pressed-earth area used for sports, games, marching, and so forth. Shiroyama, the hill with the castle on top, rose away at the side, melding into a row of more distant hills behind it. The sea was just visible beyond the grounds to the south. It was an attractive location, with a feeling of space I had found altogether lacking in the first school we had been offered, a newer one with modern buildings and all conveniences, but situated in a limited location near the centre of town. The daily journey my children would need to make would also have been much less interesting.

It was a great relief, then, when the teachers of Toyama Primary School were not only expecting my visit, but also apparently happy to offer the children a place. The headmaster was away that first day, but Mr Tanaka, my neighbour's nephew, was there waiting with the deputy head, and they were most solicitous in their attentions. They explained that they had received instructions to make us welcome from the head, who had previously taught in a Japanese school in Hong Kong and was concerned to advance the cause of international goodwill. They were slightly concerned about language, but more for communication with me than with the children, it seemed, for they relaxed visibly when they discovered I could understand their explanation of the requirements.

There were quite a number of these, as it turned out, and they were very specific. School books and other academic equipment would be provided by the school, though paid for by me, but a bag would be necessary so that homework could be carried to and fro. There was no school uniform as such, but badges were to be worn, and my younger son needed a bright yellow cap, a compulsory measure of protection for the smaller pupils as they crossed the road. Sports clothes were needed too, conforming to rather strict guidelines, and marked, visibly, with a large depiction of the child's name. A gown and hat were needed for occasional helping with school lunch, and floor cloths were to be taken for daily cleaning duties. Indoor shoes were also essential, colour-coded for class year, and again marked clearly with the owner's name. Finally, each child was required to have an earthquake hood, for emergencies.

It was vital to procure bags for all these items, partly to keep them separate from each other, but also because their programmes of transport, to school on certain specified days and home again for washing, were carefully timetabled. This could have been to avoid excessive loads, perhaps for the washing machine, but probably mostly for children's backs. They were definitely to help their owners to develop a system of order. This scheme may work eventually for Japanese children, engaged year after year in the care of their belongings, but in our case it was almost certainly more instructive for the anthropologist.

Each morning it was necessary to run through a mental check-list of requirements. There were those for daily use, depending occasionally on the time of year, those for specific days of the week, others for certain days each month – some things were allocated the first and third Thursday, for example, others the second and fourth Monday. It was also important to consult school notices, the rota for lunch duty, the timetable of extra training for the baseball club, and other sundry piles of explanatory paper that would gradually accumulate. During the two weeks of practice for a 'marathon' event in which the whole school was expected to participate, it was even necessary to mark the children's morning temperatures on a specially provided card.

Takako entered into the spirit of all the preparations, explaining the kinds of bags the children would like to carry, accompanying me to the shops to buy appropriate material – quite different for boys and girls, I might note – and she even lent me her sewing machine so that I could run them up. She bought pencil boxes for each of my boys and had them wrapped in decorative paper so that a present would be awaiting them when they arrived, but she suggested we let them choose the contents themselves. Japanese stationery shops are abundant with attractive equipment for school work and she thought, quite rightly in fact, that this would be fun preparation for their new school lives.

On 23 August, thirty-five days into my own stay in Japan, I made the journey back to the airport. It was the first time my children had flown together without me, and I was a bundle of nerves. They were to be accompanied by Jenny, although until the last minute I had not been sure that she had returned from visiting her family abroad. I had also had trouble arranging for a visa to bring someone into Japan simply to look after children, though I had couched the request in terms I hoped would appeal, about the necessity of keeping up their English education.

My arrival at the airport had also been followed by considerable panic, for although an announcement of the flight's landing appeared rather soon on the overhead board, almost immediately afterwards the notice was altered to 'delayed'. Frantic enquiries at the information desk proved useless, so I even trekked up to the observation balcony to see if I could see a crashed plane burning away on the runway. In the end, of course, after a few minutes scanning the horizon, I watched the plane land smoothly, and taxi into place. The premature arrival notice had simply been a mistake.

A Japanese friend was booked by chance on the same flight from London, and she had promised to help out if necessary. In fact, her presence did prove to be extremely fortuitous, for the arrival of two foreign children, accompanied by neither parent, was an eventuality evidently uncatered for by the rules of Japanese immigration procedure. The party was led away to an office beyond the security barrier, while I stood forlornly outside, wondering what on earth could be taking so long.

After what seemed like an interminable wait, I began to hear some strange knocking. Suddenly, in a fashion a little like the revelation of being able to see 'magic eye' pictures, I noticed that above the door I had been watching so intently was a dark glass window, evidently much better for seeing out of than into, for my children were to be dimly discerned behind it, knocking earnestly on the glass. I waved back, delighted that they had actually arrived in Japan. At about the same moment, an immigration official appeared through the door beneath. Carrying a clip-board, and with a concerned expression on her face, she walked up and asked me if these were my children. It was evidently not at all regular, in a Japanese view, to have one's offspring sent on, even with a caretaker and a Japanese friend. Once I had been located, however, we could proceed to untangle the irregularities and, in a relatively short space of time, we were making our way back to Toyama.

We had a few days' grace before school started in which Jenny and the boys could get over their jet-lag, and we began to settle into life as a family again. I purchased each of the boys a desk in which to keep their school books and resolved immediately that we would eventually take them back to England with us. They were splendid affairs constructed in light wood, with a set of shelves at the back, and several roomy drawers which slid easily in and out. Each was equipped with two electric lights, a general reading one and a stronger spotlight, and each sported a jolly scene on an area which would subsequently be made into a notice-board.

We also managed to find second-hand bicycles for each of us, including Jenny, so we made several excursions in crocodile formation to the surrounding attractions. It was still hot and sticky enough to make swimming a top priority, which we could do from the nearby beaches, but we also visited the kindergarten where we had lived before and reestablished contact with friends from our previous visit. Hamish was a major attraction since he had made quite an impact as a kindergarten pupil and he was invited to stay with an old chum.

Callum remembered nothing, but he was caught up in the general excitement of the new life, and Jenny was also soon being sought out to give English lessons to members of Takako's *nakama*. By the time the school term started, we were all feeling quite at home.

I accompanied the boys to school on the first day, which proved to be quite an experience, for me as well as for them. We started walking with the neighbourhood children, as I had understood they should do daily, but Hamish and Callum raced ahead, leaving me with the three Japanese girls. Callum was to be in Form One, and as we arrived at the school, his new teacher came out to meet him and take him into class. Hamish went up to the 4th year classroom with one of my neighbour's daughters, who happened to be in the same group, and I joined a couple of other new parents waiting to see the headmaster. Although it was September, it was not the beginning of the Japanese school year, which takes place in April, so there were only a few new families to be settled in.

The arrangement of the school offices was interesting. The head's room could be approached from the corridor, or from the staff-room, but the former route seemed barred to all but the most important visitors. The staff-room itself could be approached from the corridor, or from the office, and it seemed much more acceptable to enter directly. Once inside, however, it was organised so that only the lower-ranking teachers would be disturbed by enquiries, for their desks were placed near the door. The desks of the higher-ranking teachers were lined up in front of the head's door, although these could be approached if a lower-ranking teacher fielded the initial enquiry. The level of politeness went up too as one moved into the room, and the head was said always to receive a good measure of *keigo*, even from his former close friends.

He welcomed me most warmly, once I had run this gauntlet, offering various greetings in English, although soon relapsing into the Japanese he'd heard I could use. He asked about my work, expressing surprise, as did many, about the fact that it was I doing it rather than my husband, but he seemed rather quickly to enter into the spirit of the study. He spoke at some length about Hong Kong, and about a tour of European schools he had made, which included two days in Britain. There he had visited Eton, a school which seemed to have impressed him mostly because the pupils wore garments which in Japan are only worn for weddings. He had identified more closely with the German system of education, and he had found that though the Italians shouted a lot they seemed to get little done.

As I was to find again later, his conversation gave me food for thought. First of all, the connection he noted between the uniform of upper-class schoolboys and the ritual of a wedding was more than a flippant suggestion of coincidence, it seemed. In Japan, weddings are also times for special formalised language, virtually the same language which some Japanese people use to express their own superiority. Second, I noticed that when he asked me about my impressions of Japan I had chosen only good points (though I could have mentioned bad ones), whereas he had presented a more critical view of Europe, and he had not been slow to point out that British children do less well in mathematics than Japanese ones. Was my polite front somewhat patronising, perhaps reflecting an intrinsic (though possibly misguided) notion of superiority? And was his criticism, on the other hand, a form of defence? I had been more polite, in the British sense of the word, but I felt that his approach had been more friendly and open. I looked forward to more communication with this man.

Shortly after our interview, we moved out to the school assembly, held to mark the start of term. The head had advised me that he planned to introduce my sons to the whole school – he didn't usually do this, but because they knew no Japanese he wanted everyone to be ready to help them if necessary. The 1,200 pupils were lined up in classes in the playground, sweltering under the lingering summer heat, and a few had to be carried off, fainting, during the proceedings. The formalities were quite ceremonial, and some baseball players who had represented Japan in the United States were honoured, as were others who had won swimming competitions over the summer.

In the same style, Hamish and Callum were brought to the front of the school, stood up on the raised platform which held the head teacher, and introduced. Little was said that they could understand, but it was explained to the rest of the school that I had come from England to make a study in Japan and the boys would be spending two terms in their midst. Each person present was exhorted to treat them kindly so that when they returned to their own country they would speak well of Japan. As for the baseball players and the swimmers, the school was expected to clap, and, indeed, Hamish and Callum had been clapped by their own classes too – a clap of welcome, perhaps?

The first few days at school were mixed for the children. Hamish enjoyed the attention at first and raced off eagerly in the mornings to soak up more of it. Callum, whose blond hair stood out unmercifully amongst all the Japanese heads, found it hard to be stared at all day long and he was quite reluctant to leave home. We tried various tactics. I walked him to school myself and stood at the side of the class. The teacher walked out to meet him, marshalling a group of children to encourage him on his way. Eventually a boy whose route coincided with Callum's was detailed to meet him in the mornings, and this seemed to be the best solution. In any case, he would usually return home positive about the experience he had had at school.

He had begun to learn to write in Japanese, for example, and he was assigned fairly realisable tasks for homework. The first two characters he had to practise were interesting. They were 'up' and 'down', by themselves unremarkable, but these are the characters which, combined, describe the system of hierarchy which pervades Japanese social relations. Individually, they also qualify a number of other concepts as superior or inferior in some way – *jōhin* are high-quality goods, *gesui* is the sewerage system!

Life for Hamish did not continue as positively as it had started, unfortunately, and on the day that Callum finally ran happily into school Hamish came home early reporting that he had been involved in a fight. A few days later, his teacher rang me to say that she had sent home another boy for fighting with Hamish, but that Hamish had also been running out of the classroom. She made a point of repeating the name of this other boy quite clearly, though at that precise moment it meant nothing to me. His name was Akira.

Chapter 5

A pilgrims' trail

Some regular activities are arranged for the pursuit of examples of politeness, and wider exploration of the area reveals some ideas for further investigation.

During the early weeks of our stay, I set up a series of activities which would bring me into contact with different groups of people on a regular basis, so that I could get a feel for the dynamics of language use over time. The housewives' group to which Takako belonged was an obvious start, and they had signed up for a weekly tennis class, currently a very popular sport in the town. Six of us were enrolled, including those I had met at the initial birthday party, and a female doctor whose children had attended kindergarten with the others. This woman, Mrs Obayashi, was married into a family of doctors who ran a local practice, and I had met her husband's father and older brothers several times on my previous visit. She would arrive in an expensive sports car, and the others were somewhat in awe of her.

It was not that the others did not work, or have qualifications. Indeed, two of them had postgraduate degrees, but they had decided to put the rearing of their small children before their own careers for the time being. Obayashi-*san* employed a housekeeper to take care of domestic tasks, including some of the child care, and she also worked part-time in the hospital, but the rest of her life seemed to be taken up in activities which were not shared with the rest of the group, so there were fewer areas of overlapping interest. Of the others, two were full-time housewives, although Takako did teach a weekly English class, and two were living in houses with a family business, so they were expected to help out there as and when they had time.

The tennis coach was a dashing young man, with a smattering of

American experience, and the classes were great fun. Perhaps because he was younger than the rest of us, there was little formal language used when addressing him; indeed, the tennis court seemed to bring out the most informal communication I had heard amongst this group of well-heeled women. The coach, too, adopted a fairly intimate style of address, using endings usually reserved for children, but attaching them to shortened surnames rather than given ones. Thus, Mrs Yamaguchi, usually referred to as Yamaguchi-*san*, became Yama-*chan*, and Mrs Shimagami, more properly referred to as Shimagami-*san*, became Shima-*chan*. In my case, he just went for 'Joy', or sometimes, when I missed a shot, 'Joy, Joy, Joy!'

The tennis class was interesting in another way, for the methods of learning were rather different for me, though quite consistent with techniques used in other classes in Japan. Despite being of Western origin, this sport was treated, at least by the pupils, a little like a martial art. The teacher would demonstrate various postures, appropriate for a particular shot, as indeed he might have done in America, and members of the class would concentrate great attention on getting every detail right, down to the position of the last finger. This reminded me of the *kata* or bodily 'shapes' used by actors in Kabuki, and on the positions taught in classical ballet, also currently popular in Japan. It was undoubtedly a very effective way to learn, for my classmates made good progress, but it was interesting to observe the subtle differences in learning methods.

After the class each week, we would sit around a table and chat for a while, sipping our energy-giving drinks, such as the notorious Pocari Sweat, and putting back any weight we might have lost by eating delicacies that someone would bring along. It was a good way to get to know the members of this housewifely group, and, despite the lack of formal language to observe, I felt that my work was progressing. Actually, the language did become significant in the long-term view of things, because the occasions for informality are of course to be offset against and compared with occasions for formality, and it was eventually possible to make suggestions about why tennis should be seen as informal in this way.

In the meantime, I decided to seek out one or two more formal classes to join because teacher/pupil relations are often given as examples for polite exchanges in textbooks and manuals, and I wanted to find some cases to observe. One of the members of the original housewifely group had decided to forgo the tennis experience, and she and Takako were attending a fortnightly cooking class, which they again invited me to join. The teacher was welcoming, and there was plenty of chat to observe. Although I never really came to know the other members of the class very well, it was another good opportunity to take part in an activity which allowed me to listen to language use between other people, and, apart from my two friends, they were unaware of my interest.

The cooking was also fun, and unlike the tennis class, where my previous style and technique probably deteriorated slightly in the stringency of a learning environment strange to me, I was able to pick up some completely new skills in the preparation of food. Each week we created something delicious to eat together at the end of the lesson, and we often had a box of goodies to bring home to the family. The practices I picked up in the class were also later to influence the thinking of my research, but this I could not yet anticipate.

Members of the housewives' group were also taking lessons in knitting and Western sewing, and I went along to one of each of these, but I had absorbed these skills so early in life that I found the detailed explanations and discussions intensely tedious. I still needed to find a more formal class to observe, so I decided to try out *ikebana*, or Japanese flower arranging, and I set off one morning to look for a house I had noticed which displayed a likely-looking signboard at the gate. The house was set back from the road, approached through a neat and well-kept garden. It was a traditional wooden house, but recently rebuilt, so there was a pleasant smell of cedar as I entered the porch and called out a greeting. The teacher herself came to the door, a woman in her fifties, and she was immediately most encouraging, drawing me inside to explain the details of the classes. We sat in an immaculate purpose-built tea room, for she also gave classes in the tea ceremony, and she asked me if I wouldn't like to take this up as well. I said I would start with flower arranging, and we made an appointment for my first class.

It was still early, and as I was still becoming used to the district, I decided to keep cycling, to get a greater feel for the area, and establish some wider bearings. It was a pleasant, sunny day, but the oppressive warmth of the summer had at last eased, and I travelled quite some distance, until my surroundings became rather rural. The side of the road fell away into neatly planted rice fields, the stalks standing staunchly in their perfectly straight rows, and the delicate fronds of some tall bamboo waved in the distance. I was impressed by the number of shrines and temples I passed, and began to feel that we might also have stumbled on quite a religious part of the country. The language of priests and their parishioners would be interesting, I mused, as might be the language used to address gods.

I entered the various compounds I was passing, to have a look around, and take a break from the slight incline I was climbing. Many country shrines in Japan are used only at the times of their various festivals, and there was no one around to explain the focus of worship which each of them represented. I could sometimes read the name of the god to be invoked there, and if they were neighbourhood shrines, I could see the name of the district being protected, but I was drawn into one compound which seemed to have no such affiliation. To one side, there was a small path winding away up the hill. It seemed to be a kind of pilgrims' trail, marked with Buddhist statues which displayed numbers, and a sign at the entrance suggested that there would be 88, the number associated with Japan's most famous pilgrimage, to be found on the island of Shikoku.

In Shikoku, it takes several weeks to visit all the associated temples on foot, although people now tour them by car, or air-conditioned coach. This seemed to be a mini version, with statues at very frequent intervals, and, intrigued, I decided to follow the trail. It was quite a climb, and I soon recalled that the heat was not that far gone. I persisted in my quest, however, and was drawn further and further into the woods which cloaked the hillside. The trail led downhill again for a while, and the path seemed to curve around, but the numbers on the statues continued to climb. There was no recent evidence of offerings, and the undergrowth threatened to swallow up some of the route, which was also heavily draped with spiders' webs, but it seemed a shame to turn back, once started.

At one point I lost the track, but came across a small hut, possibly built as a retreat, and I approached it nervously in case there was someone inside. There was nothing to indicate any sign of human life, though I did hear a slight noise. The whole atmosphere was weird and lonely, and I balked at testing the evidence. Suddenly, I was surprised out of my reverie by voices, only a few yards away. I peered through a thick bamboo grove and found, to my amazement, that the path was now within sight of the main road. At first I was pleased that I would not now need to retrace the overgrown track, but it soon became clear that there was no other way out. The tiny hut was effectively surrounded by an impenetrable natural barrier. I could see the cars of the civilised world passing by, but I could only reach them by returning along the long, winding path.

When I got back to my bicycle, I was greatly relieved. I had ventured out with bare legs, now very scratched, and the experience had been somewhat unnerving. Looking more closely at the notice at the entrance to the path, which included a map of the route, it could be discerned that the course did indeed cover a rather limited area. This miniature pilgrims' trail had succeeded in reproducing a very effective impression of the distance, effort and loneliness which a real, long-distance trek must invoke, without using more than a small part of the hillside. I wondered what purpose such a path would serve, when it was used, and whether the little hut, lost in the interior, had any particular meaning.

Some workmen entered the shrine compound as I was leaving, perhaps to eat their packed lunches, so I greeted them jovially. When I mentioned that I had been around the trail, they looked surprised, and commented rather gruffly that I must have been bitten by mosquitoes. In fact, it had been the spiders' webs which had been more bothersome, but they weren't really interested in having a long chat. They seemed a little embarrassed, and they joked about me amongst themselves. They had very strong local accents, which I found hard to understand, so I felt excluded. It was noon, and I set off home.

Cycling back, I passed a large Buddhist temple, where a board displayed a notice which I could not completely decipher, but which seemed to suggest a further connection with the ancient lord Satomi, possibly the site of his grave. The temple was clearly in good order, with a well-swept compound, and neatly trimmed bushes. At the side was a dwelling house, with washing hanging on the line outside, so I thought I would stop and enquire of the housewife about the pilgrims' trail. Women's language is usually easier for me to understand anyway, and the Buddhist priest's wife would be better educated than the workmen. I called out a few times to see if anyone was at home, but there was no immediate reply.

I was about to give up when an old man appeared, dressed only in a set of cotton underwear. He was dignified, however, and quite friendly. He told me that he was the former priest of the temple. His son had now taken over, and his son's wife was out at work. His state of undress was disconcerting, however, and rather stifled the opportunity for further conversation, so I apologised and went on my way. In fact, I was to meet this man again, by chance, on two further occasions, and his whole family was later to have quite an influence on our lives.

His son turned out to be a well-known shakuhachi player, as well as a priest, and he was subsequently to invite me to a concert in Tokyo, where I heard him perform a world première of a piece by Tōru

Takemitsu, who was present in the audience. He was also to introduce me to some interesting ideas about the language of art. The 'housewife' I had sought was herself an accomplished koto player, whom I met at a concert, and she agreed for me to sit in on some of her classes and observe the language she used with her pupils. Their daughter was in the school class of my older son, Hamish, who was invited to a birthday party at the temple, and her aunt, the father's sister, whom we met on that occasion, was a local artist who displayed her work in a gallery near the station.

I might have met these people anyway, in their different contexts, but I had a definite feeling of karmic destiny with this family. My exploratory cycle ride had opened up some new lines of inquiry on the religious front, and my chance meeting with the old Buddhist priest was to become linked with some excellent new contacts in the area. The temple looked wealthy and impressive, and its connection with the legendary Satomi inspired me next to make some inquiries about local history.

Chapter 6

Shiroyama, the Satomi legend and a new look at power

Material is gathered about the historical and political background of the research location, and some contemporary parallels are observed.

The castle we had glimpsed from the 'eel shop', and passed on the way to school, was an obvious target for further exploration in the area, and it was not long before we all trooped up the hill to see it. The walk was steep, and still hot in the late summer, but the path was wide and well maintained, with steps to negotiate the sharpest inclines. The area surrounding the castle had been developed as a large municipal park, and it was landscaped to encourage visitors to enjoy as a day out. The castle itself was a major attraction, with various objects on display inside, but there were several other features, including a series of statues, a small aviary and a historical museum. The view from the summit was spectacular, with the town laid out far below, clinging to the long sweep of the coastline beyond. The school was clearly visible, and sometimes, when I took visitors up, I would imagine I could pick out two blond heads amongst the tiny figures running around in the playground. In the other direction, the houses gave way to rice fields and other agricultural developments, somewhat higgledy-piggledy in layout, but each a perfect geometric shape, with the plants in straight lines, and the edges neatly finished off. Beyond that, the hills rose up a magnificent green against the usually blue sky. The tip of the Boso Peninsula has a pleasant, temperate climate, even in winter, and this hillside park offered plenty of open space to enjoy it.

Inside the castle, we found a display of animal puppets, and several scenes from an illustrated theatrical production. The local lord, Satomi, had been made the hero of an epic novel by a well-known Japanese writer, Takizawa Bakkin, and his work had also inspired a

Bunraku, or puppet, play, a Kabuki play and a television series. The fictional characters, who were said to bear little relation to historical fact, had become the focus of tourist attention in this area, made famous through the medium of entertainment, and a large map at the bottom of the hill also directed visitors to the Satomi family grave, as well as to sites identified with well-known parts of the story. The castle itself had been constructed only a few years ago, though the name Shiroyama, meaning 'castle hill', suggested that it was the site of an original one.

At the bottom of the hill, in the historical museum, we discovered that the name Satomi was actually that of a family line, and there had been ten generations living in this area. The first had arrived from the north in the unstable warring period of the fifteenth century, and had established a headquarters a little further south. The Satomi family had had several encounters with another local family line, known as Hōjo, now the name of the central shopping area of Toyama, and their castles had been built on various sites. It was the lord of the ninth generation who had chosen the site of the present touristic reconstruction, but his castle had lasted only a few years, for his son was defeated, without issue, by the ruling Tokugawa family.

The family line was not continuous, and we learned that the fourth lord had been the younger brother of the third, who had inherited because his nephew was too young to take over when his father died. When the nephew reached the age of 18, he grew tired of waiting to take his uncle's place, so he had killed him and forcibly taken the reins of power. His triumph was short-lived, however, for he was himself assassinated by his cousin, the son of the fourth lord, who thereby secured the family line for his descendants. These were difficult times, and life was rough within and without the family. At about this point, in the sixteenth century, the country of Japan came under the relatively benevolent rule of Hideyoshi Toyotomi, and the Satomis were granted the district of Awa to administer.

Rivalry with the Hōjo family continued, however, and a battle between the two families, which features in the epic story, is now also reenacted each year at an autumn festival on the mountain. We looked forward to seeing this bit of local colour, which was said to have been invented as part of the tourist package. All this fictionalisation and festival celebration of local history makes for vivid collective memory, and helps to mould the continuing identity of the local people. The distinction between local history and legend is always somewhat tenuous at a popular level, and when novelists and playwrights enter the fray, it becomes particularly difficult to disentangle.

Two of the largest primary schools in the district are associated with these historical rivals. The first one, which we had considered and rejected, is Hōjo, and the one my children attended is Toyama, but its location beside Shiroyama gives this name to the boys' football team. The district over which these families ruled, Awa, has now become a county, which incorporates farming land, fishing communities and mountains, as well as the more populated area around the towns.

According to the museum, there are also several sites of religious importance, and the main Awa Shrine is said to be high in the overall Shinto hierarchy due to the appearance of a god named Inbeshi nearly a thousand years ago. The oldest Buddhist edifice dates back even further, to the Nara period, some 1,200 years before. Another famous temple, dedicated to the Kannon deity, is a pilgrimage site and the location of some important ritual activity, including a procession of children we had witnessed on our previous visit. I found out nothing further about the mini pilgrims' trail I had discovered, but we clearly lived in an area of some spiritual calibre. During our previous visit, I had often climbed another nearby hill to a striking red temple built into the overhanging rocks, and I had heard that the Shinto priest who looked after the shrine below was, unusually, a woman. I resolved to visit some of these religious centres during the weeks ahead.

In the meantime, however, I followed up a general interest in the town by investigating some of the contemporary structures of power and social organisation, also to find out how language might be seen to reflect relations in the land of the living. I visited the town hall, where I was given some basic local information, maps, guides, and so forth, and I interviewed a man in the tourist office who was strangely reticent about the Shiroyama development. Later I spent some time listening to discussions in the debating chamber of the local council, where political participation certainly seemed to require a facility with the polite and respectful phrases of formal speech.

The local sports day, which took place in early October, provided a good opportunity to meet the councillor for our district and his team, and they invited Jenny and me along to a couple of parties afterwards. During the day we had made complete fools of ourselves participating in all manner of sporting events, including literally biting the dust during the ever popular tug-of-war, and it was nice in the evening to drink the pain of our bruises away. There was a fairly formal gathering in the village hall, and we were then invited back to the organiser's house for a spot of karaoke. Once we had met these people, it was easier to approach them again, and I set up an interview with the councillor straight away.

He characterised our area as a very old neighbourhood, the real heart of Toyama, pointing to the site of Satomi's remains, and listing no fewer than eleven temples. Many new people had moved in now, however, and this caused some friction. He told me of a continuing court case – a land dispute between the older residents, who had customarily used a piece of mountain land, and the city which had taken it over. This dispute continued throughout our stay, and I made several attempts to get to the bottom of it, even turning up at court one day, but with little success. It didn't seem to be of any great moment, however, so I let it drop.

Jenny and I also signed up for a visit to various town facilities, a jaunt which is offered periodically to local citizens, and for which we joined a party of some twenty-eight. We saw the cauldrons in action where 10,000 school lunches are prepared – 1,000 helpings in each of ten, with four people required at any one to coordinate effective stirring, and a total of thirty employees to conduct the whole process, including delivery, collection, and disposal of the waste to a herd of local pigs. We visited a workshop employing a group of mentally handicapped people, the Community Centre, where we were treated to a lecture on general health, and the Museum, where a splendid new display had been erected on the Satomi line.

We were also taken to the Waste Disposal Centre, where we could observe, mercifully through glass, the process of disintegration of the rubbish we all put out for collection, and examine solemnly the shiny machines which convert the contents of the malodorous sewage lorries into a sparkling clear liquid that our guide proceeded to drink. This intrepid fellow took delight in his task, chastising us, as citizens, for the things we throw away, and producing a tray of watches, *soroban* (abacus), toys and other miscellaneous objects which had been removed from the human waste before it is recycled. Septic tanks were still quite widespread in Japan, and though the traditional toilet is a large, gaping hole directly over the tank, wide enough to see a fallen object floating below, one would need to be very desperate indeed to try to extract it. Our final port of call, as if to reassure us that we were not simply being provided with our own waste through the taps, was the city dam, quite a drive away up into the hills.

The whole event was hosted by the present mayor, who met us as we arrived, welcomed us to the town's facilities, and saw us off as we drove away in the town hall bus. He was a man with a large, fixed smile, and a fund of formulaic phrases which allowed little casual or even curious intervention. He used so much *keigo* that he could barely get the words through his flashing teeth, and he found more ways of thanking us for kindly coming out to see what the town had to offer than my textbook on polite language could interpret.

This man was not popular, I was told, and a forthcoming election should by rights dispose of him, but local gossip was beginning to make me aware of a level of local power which was less easy to investigate directly. It seemed that the *yakuza*, or Japanese mafia, had quite a presence in this town, and two rival groups – again – vied for backstage control of the official local politicians. Gangs such as these have a 'front' occupation, apparently, and the one currently dominant ran a local newspaper which was delivered, unsolicited, with any other papers which arrived at the house. Many of the stories were about politicians and political issues so this was clearly an instrument capable of some considerable pressure.

I understood from previous reading that control of various entertainment areas in this resort town would be part of the infrastructure such gangs would be keen to maintain, gambling being a particular forte, along with prostitution and protection. These groups were not a social clique with which I had planned to seek personal involvement during this housewifely visit, but I could hardly ignore a presence which seemed to be so powerful. The language of the *yakuza* might also be interesting, for it was said that their social organisation was the most reminiscent extant of the old samurai-type hierarchy, based on a parent–child model, and the leaders of the gangs are still known as *oyabun*, literally 'parent-part'.

It was important to be careful, however, for this underworld of a Japan otherwise renowned for its safety was characterised by an association with violence. The news bulletins which circulated the neighbourhood regularly carried warnings from the police about resisting pressure from gangland, and just over a month after our arrival it was reported in the local press that there had been an explosion outside the house of the current head, and a severed hand found at the scene. The fingerprints had made it possible to identify the injured man, who had later checked into a hospital in Tokyo, several hours' drive away. His intention had apparently been to blow up the motorboat of the local *oyabun*, but the device had gone off in his hands, and the assault had failed.

This man's house was within our immediate district, and we had probably raced against him at the sports day, I mused. On another investigative bike ride, I ventured to cycle by and have a look at the site of this violent incident. The house was built for defence – a large white construction, with no windows on the outside, and cameras positioned at the outer corner pointing down each of the approaching streets. The whole edifice was bolstered by a sloping foundation of large, shaped stones, of a variety normally only seen at castles. A large, impressive gate stood slightly ajar, revealing an inner courtyard, where a couple of expensive black cars were being polished by a burly man. The boat was vulnerable, however, for it was outside the fortress.

Whether we liked it or not, it was highly possible that we would come into contact with the local *yakuza* gang, and I decided to seek some further information. Previously, in rural Kyushu, I had been greatly aided in my research by making contact with the local police, who keep records of all the houses, their occupants and their property, and I decided to see if a similar system worked in the city. I had also heard that the police are generally well informed about *yakuza* activities, and that sometimes the two systems of control are not actually averse to helping one another.

A police box stood a short ride in the opposite direction, and I called by, unannounced. The two officers on duty took seriously my request for information about the local area, but they were cautious, and they wanted proof of my intentions. I suggested various ways of reassuring them, including an introduction from my previous friends in the town, but they decided the best plan was to make contact themselves with the old police box in Kyushu. It had been eleven years since I had lived there, and I was not able immediately to remember the name of the policeman who had helped me, but I gave them all the other information they needed about my residence there and they said they would follow it up and get back in touch with me.

True to their word, two policemen appeared on my doorstep a few days later, happy with my credentials, and willing to give me information about the area in which I now resided. I made an appointment, and later visited at a time convenient for them. Police records included information about all the residents in the area, with occupations of the men, and further information about whether their wives go out to work. They had a record of the numbers of children in each house, and the schools they attended. They knew, of course, of the criminal records of any of their charges, and they also appeared to know about the gang members in the area. Our local *oyabun* had established himself there some sixteen years previously, they explained, when he took over a large plot of land as payment for a gambling debt.

He and three *yakuza* neighbours were registered as 'without occupation', though this the police explained was probably because they had failed to cooperate with the officer who had called to collect the data. They told me about the newspaper front occupation, gave me the address of the offices, and indicated that our *oyabun* was chief to some 300 underlings. He himself was unlikely to break the law, they explained. He was a clever man, he and his wife were university graduates, and his children were sent to extra classes after school. I enquired about the ages of his children, remembering Hamish's fight, and I discovered that there was a boy in the same year as Hamish, at the same school. However, they didn't have a record of the boy's first name, and they pointed out that there were around 200 children in each year. Nevertheless, I have to say that I did begin to experience some disquiet.

Part II

Events to attend

Chapter 7

Wrapping the body
Two local festivals

Local events provide an important way for an anthropologist to get involved with people informally, though the usefulness to the research is unpredictable.

Our previous stay in Toyama had run right through the summer, and we had attended innumerable local festivals in the seaside region where we lived. Festivals in Japan may be large, spectacular affairs, advertised in the tourist literature, or they may be low-key gatherings to pay homage to a small, but nevertheless respected, shrine. Our district had a whole range to offer, starting in the early season with very localised events, building up gradually through the celebrations of larger administrative units to a final grand parade along the seafront, when each neighbourhood came out pulling a splendid, decorated float. All these occasions offer an opportunity for a break in the routine of everyday life, a release from the usual conventions of good behaviour, and, for the anthropologist, an excellent opportunity to meet local people and observe without being too conspicuous.

This time, we set up house in the early autumn, and I had been frustrated in the summer to hear the haunting sounds of the festival drums and flutes as the local children practised for a festival which I would miss whilst travelling elsewhere. Still, I had felt more sorry that my children would not arrive in time than bothered on my own behalf, as I hadn't imagined a noisy, usually fairly drunken festival to be a source of much useful information for the research project. Thus, when I became aware of two autumn festivals we would have a chance to visit, I regarded them as possible family breaks rather than serious chances to pursue my investigations. A social anthropologist is rarely on holiday, however, and each turned out in the long run to have some considerable value.

The first was a major two-day event which drew participants from all over an area about the size of an English county (*gun* in Japanese). It was held at a large Shinto shrine in central Toyama, dedicated to the powerful deity Hachiman, who is also remembered at smaller shrines in many communities. Local people from these other shrines arrive from all directions, dressed in distinctive local costume. On the first day, teams of lively youths carry in decorated portable shrines, and present them before the main shrine building, with much dancing and jumping about. On the second day, these first groups leave, and heavy floats are pulled in by people of various ages lined up along strong, heavy ropes.

The whole area was bedecked with flags and bunting, and the approaching streets were lined with rows of little stalls selling all manner of festival food and drink, a huge range of cheap toys and sweets, and helium balloons and other paraphernalia of the festival atmosphere. Some of the stalls looked sinister, indeed one seemed to be raffling unpleasant-looking guns, and their keepers are all apparently another type of *yakuza* who travel the country visiting shrines of this sort for their annual festivities. The demeanour of the male salespeople is quite recognisable: casual dress, cheerful, leering smiles and a characteristic punch-perm haircut. They were also chatty, displaying none of the Japanese reticence sometimes found in response to a foreigner in this part of the country, and I found them easy to talk to.

More interesting from the linguistic point of view, however, were the slightly varying accents of the groups of men who gathered around the back of the main part of the shrine to rest and refresh themselves after heaving in their enormous portable shrines. They tended to sit in localised groups, laughing and joking amongst themselves, as they knocked back can after can of beer, and their language was rough and difficult to understand. They were less friendly than the stall-holders, whose business it was to attract customers, but they would answer questions, if a little gruffly. The thing I noticed especially, though, was the way their language would change when they addressed anyone outside of their own group.

Here was another example of the code-switching I had learned about from Hosaka-*san* (Rehabili). The men had travelled from various parts of the county, some rural and isolated, and each group had a distinctive local dialect which they used amongst themselves. In communicating with outsiders they slotted into a more standard form of Japanese, slightly more polite, as one would expect for strangers, but not the completely standard version advocated for schools. When the conversation was with other Japanese from the same area, it still sounded like local dialect to me, but it was different from the banter of the inner circle, and I could see clearly the way language provides a kind of protective barrier around those who share a particular variety.

During the period of my stay in Toyama I had regular discussions with Takako about the language I was observing, and she would often make comments from her own experience. In this case, we were able immediately to draw a parallel with the refined language of the upper classes of Yamanote in Tokyo, who cut themselves off by using language beyond the abilities of those with less meticulous 'breeding', but Takako came up with some other interesting ideas. One related the use of language to erecting a protective barrier in circumstances of uncertainty, and she used the expression *kamaeru*, which is also found in sport as a term roughly meaning 'get ready'. In Japanese, it also has an implication of adopting a posture, quite in keeping with the reactions of fellow-members of the tennis class when we were exhorted by the coach to *kamaeru*.

Takako had noticed the way a stranger who came to her door had unexpectedly become tongue-tied when Takako spoke, and her psychiatrist husband had suggested that the visitor had been unsure how to address someone who was clearly not from the district. Under such circumstances, it would be usual to adopt a protective posture, he explained, in other words, for the person to *kamaeru*, or to construct an appropriate front. The woman had not been expecting an outsider to answer the door, so she had been caught unprepared. In fact, Takako herself usually adjusted her own language in speaking to local people, some of whom had actually commented on my previous visit on how easy she was to talk to, despite being a doctor's wife from outside the area. On this occasion perhaps she, too, had lapsed into her more formal style.

The festival-goers were in a similar situation, then, away from home and unsure exactly how best to behave. They relaxed amongst themselves, but erected a protective barrier when addressed by someone outside their group. This principle had played an important part in Japanese history, I later learned, for during warring periods, locals who protected their own discourse in this way could recognise an outsider by his or her inability to use it. Spies were thus easy to detect, unless they were disaffected locals, and it was difficult to travel *incognito*. Members of itinerant groups like the festival *yakuza* were in a powerful position, however, for they could move around the country relatively unobtrusively. This conclusion was quite encouraging, for our foreignness and its effect on language was suddenly much more relative than I had previously thought.

Another impressive aspect of this grand festival was to be observed in the clothes worn by the major participants. The youths who carried in the heavy portable shrines were all clad in white cotton, but with brightly coloured sleeves pulled up over their arms, and headbands of clear plain hues which were different for each of the villages represented. Those who pulled the floats wore predominantly black, but their jackets were the traditional festival *happi* coats, stamped across the back with the character for 'festival', and on the lapels, with the name of the shrine. They, too, wore colours to indicate their local origins. These were seen in headbands, again, but also in a kind of wrap-around top, which was worn under the *happi*.

Men, as well as women, wear make-up at festivals in this area, and younger women cavort around in their festival clothes in a fashion which would be most inappropriate for their neat, daily Western attire. There is much drinking and jollification, and individuals take turns to demonstrate their ecstasy by strenuous beating of the huge *taiko* drum attached to the back of the floats (see Figure 1). The floats themselves are strong, permanent constructions, each a collective display of local skill, carved and crafted in a distinctive design. They carry the children who beat out the constant rhythm of their particular area on the smaller drums inside, accompanied by the gentler sounds of the festival flutes. Eventually they parade away from the shrine, down the main street to the station, where they split off in the directions of their homes.

I was struck by how attractive the festival clothes made their wearers look, how much they contributed to the mood of the occasion, and how very well suited they were to the Japanese physique. As festivals do around the world, the occasion offered a chance for role reversal, outrageous behaviour and a clear break with routine, but it was also a demonstration of local identity and apparent historical continuity. The clothes are characteristic of this part of Japan, but they are also very Japanese. The *happi* coat is used abroad to stand for Japan, and it does not change in line with fluctuations of fashion. The coloured headband is worn throughout Japan to mark a ritual occasion, and the local costume is preserved to stand for the area in which it was developed.

These were haphazard thoughts at the time, and I noted them all carefully in my diary. Later they became an important part of a line of thinking that I had hardly begun to develop. Another feature of the

Figure 1 Drumming is a feature of festivals in Japan, and Hamish gets a
lesson

festival played a similar role. As we paraded away from the shrine, I
noticed that the houses in the festival district had all been literally tied
up with a thin twist of plaited straw rope, hanging along the streets
below the roofs, like a long line of bunting. These ropes, which were
punctuated regularly with tiny slips of white paper, were identical to
those I had seen used on ritual occasions to mark off a sacred area, such
as the temporary shrine set up for blessing a building site before work
starts. Here, too, they had been put up as each house was blessed for
the coming year, an integral part of festival proceedings.

Clothes featured at the other autumn festival we attended, although
this one had little to do with shrines and the sacred. Nor had it much
to do with tradition, apparently, despite its reenactment of an historical battle. It was the Shiroyama Festival, which we learned had been
created as a tourist attraction only two years previously. Some of the
same festival costumes appeared, and there was a float with festival
drums, but the overall atmosphere was altogether different and most of
the costumes had been hired from a film company. This was an occasion with no religious connections, contrived entirely for commercial
benefit, and, as it turned out, it was also an opportunity for some
municipal confidence reconstruction.

An assortment of people in ordinary apparel began to gather in the park at the bottom of the hill at the appointed time, and shortly afterwards they were rewarded with an orderly procession to watch. This consisted of teams of young samurai warriors, boys and girls, the latter armed with tall, evil-looking spears. In their midst came two lorry-floats, one carrying a princess with a mane of long black hair and an animal of indeterminate species, something between a wolf and a cat, and the other the usual *taiko* drums and a few people dressed in festival attire. The procession marched around the spacious arena which had been marked off for the occasion, and groups of warriors settled themselves around it, as if for a tournament of some kind.

Before there was any action, however, the audience was obliged to listen to several speeches by local dignitaries. There were many formulaic phrases of greeting, some self-congratulation about the construction of the castle three years before, and a rambling reminiscence about childhood play on this historically significant local mountain. Then came the 'battle'. Flares were lit, another team of soldiers arrived at the entrance to the arena, and the two sides ran to the middle. There was some shooting, several bouts of sword-play, and the newcomers, Hōjō, of course, were eventually defeated. The significance of the princess and the wolf/cat never became clear to me, or to the several members of the audience whom I probed. They referred me to the epic, however, and noted wryly that in history the outcome of the battle had been quite the opposite.

At this point members of the procession, largely made up of local children older than those of my acquaintance, set off to march up to the top of the hill to the castle, where they posed for photographs with their families. For younger children, and others who felt inclined, there was a tent where the same historical costumes could be hired for photographic purposes, and Hamish and Callum went on the celluloid records of several people present as they converted themselves into foreign-faced samurai soldiers (see Figure 2). In fact, Hamish and Callum seemed to be more of an attraction than anything else to some of those present, whose views of the festival were jaded, to say the least.

Later, when I pressed my enquiries about the organisation of this festival, I discovered some of the reasons for the apparent apathy. First of all, the construction of the tourist attractions and facilities in this area had not met with universal approval amongst the tax-payers of the city. The castle, which represented only a short period of local history, had been expensive to construct, and its contents were less than scintillating. It was in fact a branch of the museum which had been completed a year later, and its connection with a fictional reconstruc-

Figure 2 Callum dressed up for a photograph
at the local historical festival

tion of events seemed somewhat inappropriate to the more historically minded citizens. Finally, and this was perhaps the main explanation for the mixed feelings on the day we attended, a serious accident to a local teenager had marred the occasion the previous year.

The festival continues, at the expense of local unions representing various forms of tourist accommodation and souvenir shops, with a grant from the city. The 'traditional' float is provided by a drumming preservation society, and the clothes are hired from a company in Tokyo. This autumnal occasion is actually one of a series associated with the smart new developments in Shiroyama Park. In the spring, there continues an older festival to celebrate the flowering of a wonderful display of azaleas which covers the hillside, which we had enjoyed on our previous visit. In mid-summer, a Noh play is performed by firelight in front of the castle, and in September, when the weather is clear, there is a 'harvest moon-viewing', with musical accompaniment by koto players, cancelled that year because of dense cloud.

In fact, I had been luckier than expected that day for I did see the moon. Takako had gathered some grasses to decorate her house for the event, and prepared some special food, but because the music was cancelled, we simply shared the tea and went about our lives. Afterwards I had set off to the supermarket to do a bit of shopping, and, just as I came out, there was a magical break in the clouds and the enormous moon rose magnificently above the horizon. I had not until that moment believed the tales of the size that the harvest moon attains, nor indeed understood why a celebration should be built around it. This time, I was the one no one believed, for despite my immediate and amazed conversion, I could find no one else who had witnessed the wondrous glimpse.

As a tourist, this experience would go down as a highlight of my visit, and the Shiroyama Festival certainly provided me with some striking photographs, and a fun day out for the boys. As an anthropologist, nothing exists in a personal vacuum, and the episodes shared with local people are the moments which count. These two festivals had been very different occasions, the one full of spontaneous joy and celebration, despite the clear evidence of complicated organisation and coordination, the other more contrived and controversial. But then, perhaps it just depends to whom one talks. Festivals were not my subject of study, and had they been, I would have become much more engaged. In practice the first at least still offered some insights which later became very valuable.

Chapter 8

The housewives' 'Club for Life'

Interviews are set up, but the daily round of activities also proves to be valuable for the research, as do special occasions which arise.

Interspersed with these special events, domestic life had settled into a relatively predictable routine. School activities required serious attention, first in the morning in the preparation of the appropriate bags for the day, and, later, when the boys returned, even Callum often had exercises to complete at home. These were relatively straightforward, perhaps describing his family, or practising a couple of characters or an easy set of sums. Hamish's class had more complicated homework, which was still beyond his Japanese reading ability, but his teacher took seriously his general socialisation to class life and she used the little notebooks they all carried to and fro to indicate things I should explain to him and reinforce.

Jenny took care of the basic housekeeping, adopting the Japanese practice of sweeping the wooden floors and *tatami* matting each morning, and getting the day's laundry through the washing machine and out onto the line. She took pleasure in preparing meals, investigating new ingredients she could find in the local shops, and generally making friends with the storekeepers. The fishmonger was a regular port of call, and we enjoyed a huge range of produce made possible by our proximity to the fishing community. While Jenny was building up her vocabulary, we went together to seek new specimens, and marvelled at the care and efficiency with which our selections were washed and prepared. Once she had the domestic tasks under her belt, Jenny, too, took up a class – in ink painting – and she continued to respond to requests to give English lessons.

A regular event in the life of my housewives' circle was the ordering and collecting of a range of direct purchases through an organisation known, after the English, as the 'Co-op'. This was a kind of club, joined by the investment of a sum which contributed to the fairly minimal administration, and involving weekly trips to an empty plot adjacent to a nearby apartment building where the goods were delivered. Members of the local division would gather at the appointed time, split into smaller sections to arrange makeshift tents as protection against the sun, and when the delivery truck arrived, they would form a human chain to unload and distribute the purchases. In the tents, these would be unpacked and checked, and each member would pick up the goods they had ordered.

A large and fairly complicated form provided the means of ordering, and this would appear each week to be filled in and dispatched. The goods available included a range of seasonal produce, which necessarily varied from week to week, and a series of regular items such as eggs and dairy products. There was also a small section of non-food items, such as toothbrushes, paper towels and other household aids. The main purpose of the club was to order fresh food directly from the producers, however, and much of it was organically prepared. This club was part of a movement, originally set up by housewives frustrated at the fluctuating price of milk, to gain more control over their supplies.

It was also a way in which the household manager could monitor the nourishment she provided for her family, and this was a serious issue amongst my professional housewives. During pregnancy a woman in Japan receives a fair amount of literature about her own health and that of her developing foetus, and many follow this interest up for years by reading all the latest magazines and books about nutrition and health. Schools and kindergartens which provide food send home a list of the menus for a month at a time, with detail about precise content and calorific value, and a serious housewife builds this into an overall plan for the whole family. Putting a weekly order into the Co-op is therefore quite in keeping with this degree of planning. My housewifely skills were greatly inferior in this respect, so our orders sometimes arrived at times which did not fit in with Jenny's projected menus, which could pose a problem in the hot weather. However, several benefits arose from my involvement in this group. First, it gave me great insight into the lives of the professional housewives with whom I worked, and the degree of planning in which they engaged. I learned a lot about the minute details of a Japanese quality of life which is sometimes overlooked, especially by foreign feminists who apply their own standards to a system they see as oppressive. A large cooperative group of this sort, known as the Seikatsu Club, or 'Club for Life', was actually awarded a Swedish alternative Nobel-type prize, known as the Right Livelihood Award, for their activities.

The system they had established was seen as an important antidote to a different kind of oppression, namely that of the capitalist market, which shrouds much of the production of life's vital ingredients in the trappings of a complicated series of middlemen, wholesalers and retailers, so that finding the precise source of one's food becomes an almost impossible task. The housewives who set up these cooperative clubs made direct contact with selected farmers and horticulturalists, and installed a network much more transparent and therefore acceptable to their members. It is a kind of alternative economy, but, ironically, it may well eventually undercut the businesses in which some of their husbands are engaged, and it was, of course, the salaries of these husbands which allowed the women the time to establish the network. The need for time to participate in the activities of the Co-op Clubs caused Japanese working women and feminists to complain for a while, but the institution of evening deliveries later helped to resolve this problem.

Another advantage of belonging to the Co-op was the opportunity it gave me to meet a wider group of people on a regular basis. For example, I made one set of friends through this connection who invited us around as a family, including Jenny, engaged us in various recreational activities, such as tennis, and introduced me to a side of Japanese life I would not otherwise have encountered. The father of this family, the Hondas, worked in a children's home, which he later arranged for me to visit, and his wife took us out to meet some friends who ran a diving school. This latter activity was a jovial family concern, administered by a group of adult siblings, whose young apprentices shared their large, rambling house, and took meals with the already abundant children.

At the Co-op I also met an old contact from my previous research period, one Mr Noda, who had then been the only man working in the city's nursery schools. This time Noda-*san* was the only man amongst the housewives collecting their Co-op deliveries, and he approached me cheerfully, recognising my face more quickly than I did his after a five-year gap. He explained that he had now given up his job at the nursery and he was taking care of his own young son, who was with him, while making preparations for a *pension* he was hoping to build. His wife was still a full-time school teacher, but she planned eventually to give this up too, and together they would run the business. A *pension*, he explained, is a seaside family hotel, built in the European style and therefore taking its name from the French.

In a world where security is so highly prized, Noda came across as a wonderfully happy-go-lucky fellow. Tall and slightly balding, he stood out clearly from the female company he seemed wont to keep, but expressed neither doubts nor any particular pride in his unusual roles. Back in the day nursery he had cheerfully demonstrated the best way to teach a toddler to use the potty; now he was full of advice about the relative merits of the various Co-op products. He was committed to a high quality of life, and prepared to invest considerable time and effort into achieving it. He aspired to attain a practical ideal that others merely talked about, and was prepared to take risks and follow a dream.

At that time he was engaged in making furniture for the *pension* they would open. He wanted a particular kind of furniture, somewhat Swedish in character, with broad, bold lines and made of light-coloured wood. He had not been trained as a joiner, and he had had to learn the trade from scratch, but he was doing pretty well on the collection of chairs they would need. They also wanted to serve especially good food to their guests, and an old friend who had become a chef was living with them, trying out various dishes they would serve. Staying in the Noda *pension* would be a total experience, and another friend, an artist, was busy designing details of the décor. They also planned to hold concerts there two or three times a month.

Noda-*san*'s concern with the quality of the living environment he aimed to create reminded me of the way Mrs Takahashi had originally introduced me to White Lily Kindergarten. It was again purpose-built, largely of a kind of rustic timber, and she had clearly considered its aesthetic qualities alongside the practical aspects of moving fairly large numbers of children between their various activities. She pointed to a lack of the bright colours which often characterise kindergartens, and emphasised the use of natural materials. All the features of the play area had been carefully chosen to create an atmosphere harmonious not only with the buildings, but also with the luscious green hillside which rose away behind it.

The kindergarten uniform was also carefully designed. Each child arrived in a smart navy-blue smock, relieved at the neck with a crisp white collar, and topped with a small matching hat. The children carried identical lighter-blue shoulder bags, and sometimes a yellow carrier bag with their artwork. As they arrived, they were expected to stow these bags in purpose-built box shelves, and change into yellow play-smocks. The changing areas were equipped with neat rows of hooks, so the overall impression of a visit to the kindergarten, with or without children, was one of order and aesthetically pleasing combinations of colour and shape. The teachers contributed to this effect by dressing in trim, cheerful clothes, casual but clean and unblemished.

Mrs Takahashi's careful use of language seemed to fit in with this attention to the detail of the general environment, and I feel sure that she monitored the general appearance of her employees as well as her young charges. She herself had her clothes made by a dressmaker, and she was always immaculately turned out. She also trained her staff in the use of *keigo*, as I confirmed when I went to interview her. As Mrs T had been a chief influence in my choice of research topic it seemed appropriate to come clean with her about my intentions and seek her opinion. The book from my previous visit had just come out, so I made an appointment, and took her a copy. I was still a little nervous, for, if anything, my own *keigo* had diminished in quality. Few people in Toyama use the various speech levels with as much skill as Mrs T does, and I felt out of practice.

In fact, she was quite relaxed. Perhaps because I was no longer a mother with a child in her care, a tenant and a neighbour, she could lower her guard a little. Perhaps as the author of a book featuring her kindergarten I had elevated my status. Either way, there was less of an atmosphere of competition, and she was most cooperative. She explained almost immediately that she uses different language for parents and for teachers, and different language again for the bus drivers who work for her. She also changes her language to her employees when parents are present, increasing the level of politeness and softening her tone of voice. It is important for language to sound nice, she explained, and to get people to do things smoothly.

This was just the sort of thing I was after, and I pressed her to elaborate. She did at some length, and I learned a lot about the manipulative power of *keigo*. It soon became clear that variation in the use of language is vital, and must be adjusted to the expectations and abilities of the other. She had known one of her bus drivers since childhood, for example, so it would sound cold and distant if she were too polite with him. Instead, she addressed him rather informally, sometimes brusquely, depending on how quickly she wanted the job done. A firm order is likely to achieve a speedier response than a polite request, she explained, but she emphasised the importance of the tone of voice too. Occasionally she would raise the politeness level purposely to sound a little cold.

A degree of distance could be effective, and she talked of the rather stiff and formal language she used for making arrangements. With the head of the PTA, for example, too much *keigo* would waste time, so she dropped in only the occasional polite phrase to maintain a general overall level of decorum. At meetings of the PTA, too, one needed to be businesslike. During this stay I was invited to some of the PTA activities and I was amazed at the amount of time and effort the parents were prepared to put into their preparation. Already paying the fairly stiff fees that White Lily charged, mothers would still spend weeks on end creating arts and crafts to be sold for kindergarten funds at the annual Bazaar, and hours of their evenings practising skits for the spring concert. Was this enthusiasm created by language, or just by the immense seriousness and enthusiasm with which Mrs T took the care of their children?

No clear and unambiguous answer would ever emerge to a question as nebulous as this, of course, but Mrs Takahashi's concern with the minutiae of quality in the training of her pupils was shared by mothers who had chosen the role of the 'professional housewife'. As well as evaluating the nutritional and calorific content of the food they offered their children, great attention was also paid to the aesthetic presentation of the dishes placed before them. Packed lunches were treated almost as works of art, and one of my most humbling moments during the previous stay had been on a kindergarten outing when our hastily assembled rolls and ham had been revealed alongside the dainty creations other mothers had prepared. Perfectly formed sushi could be passed around among the assembled party, too, unlike our buns and packets of meat.

Even a casual cup of tea or coffee would be laid out in a formal fashion at the homes of my housewifely *nakama*. The cup and saucer seemed to face a particular way, the spoon irritatingly appearing at the opposite side to that expected by my English upbringing, and tiny containers of milk and sugar would be placed at the side of each. Biscuits and cakes would be individually wrapped, and these, I knew from the supermarket, cost twice as much as the ones which were purchased, open, in a packet. The quality of the beverage itself was measured rather in terms of its brand name than its flavour, but Takako had an endearing habit of lacing tea and coffee with Bailey's cream liqueur which made all this attention to detail pleasantly acceptable!

When I invited Mrs Takahashi to a meal, together with a young Oxford student she had taken under her wing, I was glad to be able to hire the charming upstairs room at the 'eel shop' for the occasion. All the necessary attention to detail was paid as a matter of course by my accomplished restaurateur and his staff, and I could concentrate my attention on our conversation. We ordered on my recommendation (in fact the only variety we had tried to date, but it seemed to be fine), and the dishes were served in elegant lacquer boxes. At the end of the meal, I could usher my guests across the threshold, where we admired the coloured carp swimming beneath us in a shimmering pool, and wave off their taxi before returning to settle the account discreetly afterwards. The expense of the occasion was easily worth more than the wriggly fish we had eaten.

Chapter 9

Cubs, sports and a shock

Attempts are made to widen the range of research respondents, a family link proves fruitful, and the importance of keeping careful notes in the diary is emphasised. They may adopt an unanticipated meaning later.

Mrs T was a valuable informant, but she was well known in the town as an astute businesswoman, and White Lily Kindergarten was the only private one for miles around. It was an unusual place, and while I could learn about the use of language, clothes and space for creating a distinctive, somewhat superior atmosphere, I needed to put this material in a broader context. My professional housewives were also of an upper-income bracket, and they chose White Lily for their children, as might be expected. Private schools did not exist at the primary level in this town, however, so my own children were now a conduit to meeting a range of other parents. I responded enthusiastically to calls to help weed the playground, and clean 'the high places' in the classroom, but in the end I was surprised by how much I learned through their leisure activities.

Hamish was an enthusiastic cub at home, and we decided to seek out the local troop. They were called 'cub-scouts', and they rapidly and earnestly welcomed us both, mother and son, into their midst. Our initial enquiry was soon followed by a formal visit from two immaculately turned-out scout leaders, keen and trim in their shorts and long socks. They put our rather casual home to shame, but I invited them into the *tatami* matting area and did my best to kneel to attention. Hamish was less impressed by these much more serious versions of the friendly River Cubs in Oxford, and he fooled around, refusing to put on any of the politeness he had surely learned. They seemed unperturbed, however, agreed that he could become a 'guest cub' during his stay, and gave me details of the next meeting.

This was a display of magic by various cubs, and Hamish made initial contact by attending, though he insisted I go with him, and there were several other parents present. Soon afterwards I received a telephone call from one of these, Mrs Sugita, the mother of the leader of the 'six' he was to join. She invited us to meet the other members of the group, parents and children, at a café in the centre of town. This was the beginning of a fruitful series of meetings for me, for the Cub Scouts of Japan (or at least the Toyama branch) seemed unable to carry out their activities without the active presence of their mothers. We prepared for, set up and served at a bazaar stall, which one might expect to do in Britain, but we also went along to a 'cook-out', where we did most of the cooking, and a kite-flying event, where we did much of the flying!

This seemed somewhat paradoxical, since in Britain cubs are trained to be independent to the point of parental worry at times, but then British parents drop their children at school on a regular basis, an act of dependence which is formally forbidden in Japan. Even the smallest children are expected to walk to school, in all weather, though they form neighbourhood groups to do it. This kind of cooperative activity seemed to me to be the epitome of the Baden-Powell ideal, and, indeed, children in Japan spend much of their lives responding to the demands of a collective conscience. At school, for example, much work is accomplished through the joint efforts of a group of five or six classmates, and these groups also take on the organisation of quite sophisticated events.

For 'cub-scouts', life seemed to be largely fun and play, but then if ordinary life is instilling the ideals of the scout movement, the meetings can perhaps take on a different role, and this apparently didn't become very serious until the boys graduated to the scouts proper. In any case, joining the 'cub-scouts' was definitely a minority activity, and they didn't even meet that often. For me, the great advantage was the varying language I could observe. Sugita-san was originally from Tokyo and her language was extremely polite, the other mothers were local and they used much plainer forms, especially when Sugita-san was out of earshot. While the others found Sugita-san somewhat affected, she felt herself to be living in a foreign country.

This spontaneous interaction was extremely valuable to me. In a ready-made group, where I had no need to explain my presence, I could observe behaviour and listen to gossip to my heart's content. I decided, after some time, that Sugita-*san*'s feeling of alienation was related to her inability to adjust her language, or code-switch, as the technical term goes. Unlike Takako, who dropped her *keigo* amongst her Toyama neighbours, and received praise for 'fitting in', Sugita-*san* persisted with her Tokyo levels of politeness, and felt distant.

Later interviews with local people confirmed my assessment of the situation, for many of the ordinary residents, unlike those who chose to send their children to White Lily, were even rather unclear about what *keigo* is. They had their own ways of notching up their politeness, but they only used the more formal version for ritual occasions. To them, those who used it in ordinary conversation sounded affected or 'stuck-up', and an inability to reciprocate inhibited the development of intimacy. Inappropriate use of *keigo* sounds cold and distant, and those in a position to adjust their language may use it to deter an overly friendly approach – or simply to turn away a salesman.

Hamish came along to the cubs, but they were not a major part of his life. He became much more involved with the Shiroyama soccer (*sakka* in Japanese) team, which scooped him soon after we arrived. Our presence coincided with the World Cup year in which Maradonna caused a scandal with an infamous handball which lost England a vital match, and Hamish was incensed to find a picture of Maradonna in pride of place on a school notice-board. He tore it down angrily and, apparently, threw it out of the nearest window. The teachers were extremely patient with their foreign charges, probably at the behest of their internationally minded headmaster, and they didn't make a fuss. I was advised of the incident in the commuting notebook, and when I explained the reasons for Hamish's act, which had not been clear in a Japan only beginning to take an interest in football, he even became something of a hero.

The soccer team trained twice a week before school, from 7 to 8 a.m., after Saturday morning school, for three-and-a-half hours, and on Sunday, from 8:30 to noon. They had an attractive black-and-white uniform, and they went off to play matches with other local teams about once a month. Relations with the boys in the team were sometimes a little tempestuous, possibly because Hamish was on occasions selected over older boys to captain their side, probably more for his novelty value than for any leadership qualities. Since Hamish was old enough to take himself to his soccer commitments, I didn't have much to do with the other parents until later – perhaps quite thankfully, as it turned out.

Callum was too young to join the soccer club, but a conversation with some parents I met at an early meeting suggested that he would be welcome to take up baseball. There was a thriving, successful squad which met at the school, and they recruited boys from the first year. Their training was even more rigorous than that of the soccer team. They met daily, before school, at 6 a.m., continued for another couple of hours after school, and, on Sunday, they trained from 7 a.m. to noon. This team, the Toyama Little Angels, had created the boys we had clapped at the opening ceremony for representing Japan in America, and one of their mothers, Mrs Yamada, had called on me to ask for help with a letter of thanks to her son's 'home-stay' family.

Mrs Yamada was also the treasurer, and I approached her to discuss the details. I was unsure whether Callum would be up to such a rigorous regime, and whether it was worth investing the quite substantial expense for equipment and uniform for only a couple of terms. The programme was somewhat modified at this early age, she assured me, and she identified a slightly older boy who would probably be willing to pass on his uniform, on loan. Both of my boys were keen to acquire the bats and gloves for themselves, so we struck a compromise, and in fact they continued their interest in baseball for some time after we returned to England, joining with American friends, and later making contact with the Japanese school in Milton Keynes. In the meantime, Callum would turn up on Sunday morning at 7 a.m.

Mrs Yamada was friendly, and we continued to talk for sometime. She had three boys of her own, and she revealed that they had taken a special interest in Hamish and Callum and their presentation on the first day of school. They were themselves a Korean family, and one had asked, on returning home, why they had not been given this kind of treatment. He wondered whether he should use his own Korean name, Lee, instead of the Japanese name, Yamada, which the family had chosen for convenience since they lived in Japan. In fact, the question of Koreans living in Japan was a political issue of some note at the time, for several had been campaigning vigorously against the way they were expected to register as foreigners even though their families had lived there for generations.

The general impression I had received from the press was that Koreans were treated rather badly in Japan. Many of them had been brought there to carry out menial tasks during the Japanese occupation of Korea, and there were now several communities whose living conditions were substantially lower than those of their Japanese neighbours. Despite their more or less permanent settlement, and the fact that subsequent generations had been born and brought up in Japan, citizens of Korean extraction were still regarded as 'aliens', required to register their fingerprints with the police, and apply to return to the country when they travelled abroad. These are the conditions under which any foreigners are granted residence, and, as I had learned when securing Jenny's visa, it is not always an easy situation.

What was interesting in the case of Mrs Yamada was that this family seemed to be treated rather well by their Japanese friends and neighbours. She had herself been born in Japan, as had her parents, and she explained that she could have chosen to become Japanese, had she so wanted. In fact, her marriage to another Korean had been arranged by her family, and although they did not speak the Korean language, they visit Korea quite often. It was thus their choice, as Koreans, to maintain their identity, and this choice influenced their relationship with local bureaucracy, as much if not more than the pressure from the Japanese system in which they lived. Mrs Yamada did not feel that she experienced the kind of discrimination, or apathy, I had unearthed in my own neighbourhood.

Their use of a Japanese name could have helped, because it meant that not everyone recognised their Korean identity, but I suspect there was more to it than this. First, the Yamadas, or Lees, were reasonably wealthy. They ran a successful family business, and they lived in a good neighbourhood. They were also upright citizens whose children excelled at school, even representing Japan in sport, and they contributed to local activities. Mrs Yamada's role as treasurer of the Toyama Little Angels was a voluntary, unpaid service, albeit with benefits to her children, but her selection indicated a degree of trust. In fact, the Yamadas behaved like Japanese in a Japanese context. Their language was appropriate, their clothes were smart, and they lived in a nice house. Only amongst their Korean friends and relatives did they behave as Koreans.

The power of an ability to adapt was again clear. Those Korean Japanese whose economic resources were less stable were at a disadvantage, of course, and growing up in a Korean neighbourhood would not help their prospects of integration, if that was what they wanted. Seen from an outside point of view, the Koreans who were politically active were complaining about their treatment, and discrimination was part of this, but had they not also chosen to be Korean, rather than take Japanese nationality? Indeed, integration may not have been their aim. In this case, the situation was more complicated than it had at first seemed. The Lees, or Yamadas, had worked out a compromise which was not yet entirely clear to their children.

All these casual conversations were recorded in my diary, which I wrote religiously every evening, or, if I was too tired, first thing the following morning. If I held a formal interview, it was written up in a different place, for it fitted with my preconceived ideas about how my research would proceed, but anthropological fieldwork is often unpredictable, and it is important to keep a record of ideas which may eventually have some bearing on the outcome. Mrs Yamada's case was not hugely influential in the long run, but it was part of a process of rethinking which was soon to come to a head, though I had no way of knowing it at the time.

I had found several examples of the way language, clothes and demeanour were effectively drawing boundaries around people, not an earth-shattering finding in itself, for it happens everywhere. The people who could adapt their language, and other markers, were in a much more powerful position than those who could not, however, and this was more intriguing. I had started out taking an interest in language for this very reason, but I was beginning to think more seriously about some of the other markers as well. Clearly, a house, or a car, is a good marker, and I thought of the way my *yakuza* neighbours chose to present themselves. I resolved to drive past their district again.

An opportunity soon arose, as it turned out, for Callum asked me to accompany him to his first baseball practice, and I made a diversion on the way back. We had received the uniform, a neat outfit in white, trimmed with navy blue, and marked boldly with the name of the team. We had made an expedition to the local sports shop and acquired, at great expense, the bat and glove, and a few practice throws had been accomplished. On the Sunday morning, Callum woke at 5 a.m., so excited was he about this new adventure, and after a few vain attempts to get him to settle, we got up and made the necessary preparations. Hamish decided to get up and come along to this momentous first meeting, although football didn't start for another hour-and-a-half, and we rode off on our bikes.

The initial warm-up set the tone, for the boys were encouraged to make several laps of the school, at some speed. When the coach arrived, they all raced to his side, and bowed formally, before entering enthusiastically into an exercise routine. We left them practising throwing, and as Hamish still had time to kill, he came with me to have another glance at the *yakuza* house. We would look somewhat suspicious standing outside staring, so we just drove casually by, and I indicated the cameras to Hamish as they came into view. Evidently we had been picked up by them, too, however, for as we proceeded gently down the road, we heard a voice calling after us.

'Hamish-*kun*, Hamish-*kun*, aren't you coming to football?' Hamish glanced back and recognised his teammate, Akira, now also a good friend. He called back an affirmative reply, but he didn't stop cycling. So Akira, his early adversary, was indeed the son of the local *oyabun*. We had considered the possibility, but we were somewhat stunned to find it to be true. Later, when we reached home, Hamish recalled meeting Akira's older brother, who had behaved in an unusually threatening manner during play in the park. In fact, it was hardly surprising that the two should be thrown together. Akira's family was well known in the district, and other children may have been warned off becoming too close. Hamish knew no better, and they were both outsiders in their own way. Still, it was something of a shock.

Chapter 10

Suicide, funerals and the well-wrapped gift

Shocking or distressing circumstances arise during the course of research, but one of these turns out to be associated with an unexpected deep insight.

It was indeed a shock to discover my son's proximity to the family of one of the most powerful men in town, even if unofficial, but it was also quite exciting. As a parent, I had occasion to meet other parents, notably mothers, and it seemed to offer another apparently innocent way to make useful observations. I also had a list of school class home telephone numbers, for the parents of each form operated a system of disseminating information, somewhat like the circulating notice-board, where they received and passed on the news in a fixed order. In fact, it was Callum's class that first introduced me to the mechanics of this ingenious arrangement.

It was on the evening of the elusive harvest moon that the mother whose name was prior to mine on the list telephoned to tell me that the father of one of Callum's classmates had died. She gave me details of the 'sending-off', but said that I was not obliged to attend. Since the average age of the parents of this class was probably between late twenties and mid-thirties, at most, I asked if the man in question had been ill. She replied in a slightly evasive fashion, claiming to be unsure of the details, but that he was probably ill. I telephoned the next person on the list, and passed on the details. She did not ask how he had died, so I had no need to perpetuate the unclear part of the information, which could have attained the value of a Chinese whisper and fouled up this useful Japanese system of communication.

I decided that the best way of expressing condolences would be to attend this 'sending-off', which seemed to be a local word for the more austere-sounding 'funeral', and it could also be useful for my research. A ceremony of any sort is delivered in appropriate language, which would certainly be formal and polite, and it was not often possible to attend a funeral inconspicuously. I contacted a couple of other mothers to see if they would be attending, and to find out about the appropriate etiquette, gift procedure and attire. A group of us arranged to go together, so we set up a meeting place and time, and one offered to drive us over to the family home, where the funeral would be held.

In the meantime, Takako had her ear to the ground, and she discovered through her own contacts that the man in question had committed suicide. The family was playing this down, however, so it was not necessarily common knowledge, and she was not sure whether I should attend. Nevertheless, the arrangements had been made, so changing them would be more conspicuous than going along, though we thought it might be prudent to appear reluctant on arrival. In fact, the other women in the quite large group which turned up were extremely reassuring. None seemed to know the family very well, a couple were not even wearing black ('It isn't a relative or anything, so I didn't bother with make-up,' said one; 'I just washed my hair,' said the other).

The overall impression was one of conformity in dress, however, for all the other women wore black, which contrasted strikingly with the white uniforms worn by most of the men present, as the deceased was a sailor in the Japanese naval defence forces. The latter sat in neat rows, but seats had not been provided for the women present, and we stood awkwardly, first at the front of the apartment building, and then in a group at the back where the main room opened out to reveal an altar set up inside. The coffin was laid out in front of this, with a photograph of the man in pride of place, neatly tied up with criss-crossed black ribbon. The close relatives sat in front of the coffin: his wife, the small boy and the man's parents.

The order of proceedings moved from a period of chanting by the Buddhist priest, to a formal speech by the chief officer of the unit, through the emotional recollections of a representative of the age-mate group. Everyone present then filed up, in rows of five, to take a pinch of incense from a large container and add it to the burning pile in front of the photograph, a symbolic gesture of farewell. We then returned to the front of the building, where we waited to see off the coffin, which was carried out following members of the family, each holding an item of the accompanying utensils. The father of the deceased made a final speech of thanks for such a splendid funeral, and the entourage was driven away to the crematorium.

The speeches did not entirely give away the cause of death, although both the commanding officer and the age-mate were full of sorrow and some remorse, it seemed. Since I knew that it was a case of suicide, I could pick up some of the insinuations, but it may not otherwise have been clear. The commanding officer mentioned that he had grown thin, for example, and that they had tried reducing his workload, but, he apologised, they had not been able to help. The age-mate apologised, too, addressing the dead man directly, as if he were still there to speak to and reply. Finally, the father apologised for the trouble they had caused to the neighbours, thus taking responsibility as a family for the events which had taken place.

The other mothers said nothing directly about the cause of death, commenting most audibly on what a nice person the mother was, and how sad for the child. The mother was a contemporary of the class teacher, Mrs Okazaki, whom they noted was only 29 years old. However, there was some muttering amongst them which suggested that there was at least a suspicion of suicide, although one commented, fairly loudly, that 'it is not the kind of thing you can ask'. Another disagreed, that 'one should ask', but neither specified out loud what 'kind of thing' they were talking about. Presumably as I was a fairly bumbling foreigner, I was not consulted, so I was able to keep my own knowledge to myself.

It was an interesting exercise in the expression of 'front' and 'back' knowledge, which are clearly distinguished in Japanese society, to the extent that an inability to make the appropriate distinctions can be seen as a sign of mental illness (or foreignness, of course). It was probably inappropriate for me to ask the cause of death on the telephone, but the 'front' reply, that he must have been ill, was a suitable compromise between the whole truth and a cover-up. If the man committed suicide, he could well have been ill, I suppose, although there are more noble reasons for taking one's own life in Japan. If there had been one of these, it would have been a matter of public knowledge, however, so the answer was quite diplomatic – assuming my informant was herself aware of the situation, which, of course, she might not have been.

The details of the ceremony were also interesting, and I noted them all in my diary, although I would not come to fit them into a wider scheme until much later.

Not long afterwards, I had another opportunity to observe the ritual surrounding death when the father of an old friend in Tokyo passed away, this time through natural causes and general old age. I could observe at first hand the reactions of the immediate family this time, for I had visited them before, and the mother remembered me well. I had met Mr Tamaru during my first visit to Japan some fifteen years previously, when we lived in the same house, a community of some ten Japanese and a couple of English-speaking foreigners. We, the foreigners, were expected to speak English during supper each evening, so that our Japanese house-mates could practise their language skills, but it had also been an excellent opportunity for me to learn idiomatic Japanese, and to make a number of good friends.

I had met Tamaru-san many times over the years. We always had a drink or a meal when I was in Tokyo, and we compared notes as our lives progressed. We discussed our respective marriages, as they occurred, and sent presents to one another's children, visiting them too when this became practical. Now it was bereavement, and Tamaru-san opened his heart. He lived in a different part of Tokyo from his mother, but he was the eldest son, and was suddenly aware of the responsibility of being the oldest male in the family. He would have to decide, with her, what to do about the family home, and how she would live with only half the pension they had received when her husband was alive. Many Japanese families move in together at such a time, or into a new house on the family land, neatly divided into two apartments. He thought he might prefer to be a short walk away. He was clearly deeply affected by losing his father, and would miss him a lot. Discussing the practical arrangements was a way of expressing this loss.

I could not attend the funeral this time, but Tamaru-san took me to visit his mother, and the family altar where they had lain the ashes and set up a black-trimmed photograph. I had consulted a few people about an appropriate gift, and a pretty large sum of money seemed to be one possibility, suitably wrapped in a funeral envelope. It should be placed upside down, I was told. Otherwise, a basket of fruit might be accept-able, and I decided on the latter, feeling that money was very impersonal, although this does seem to be the more common solution. The fruit was wrapped in special paper, with the funeral motif of lotus leaves and a printed black band, and as we entered the house, I was ushered straight to the cushion before the altar, where I laid down my gift. With a little guidance, I tapped a gong to summon the spirit, lit some sticks of incense, and folded my hands in prayer. This was a way to pay respects, and say goodbye to Mr Tamaru senior.

His wife, my friend's mother, thanked me for the fruit, pointing out that her husband had liked fruit so it was a good gift, and we talked a little of the last time I had visited. After a while we moved through to the living-room, where we chatted long into the night, and she revealed a stunning memory about my life and family. She was clearly glad to have a visitor, and asked me to stay, which I did. She was thin and drawn, and the house had been neglected, so I was glad if I could offer a little comfort. I think a foreign friend is sometimes a relief for Japanese caught up in the restrictions of social constraints – indeed, perhaps for anyone. There are fixed words for expressing sympathy at a time such as death, and a clear procedure, but a foreigner may be treated less formally.

When it came time to go to bed, Mrs Tamaru took me back into the best room, where the urn of ashes was displayed, and she pulled some futons out of the cupboard. I was to sleep in the presence of the honoured dead, and she stacked several mattresses as if to compensate. She indicated a huge pile of black and white envelopes in which they had received monetary gifts, and hoped I wouldn't feel bad surrounded by these things. I commented that it must be comforting that so many people remembered him, but she said she would feel better if they were red and gold, the colours for gifts associated with happy occasions. In fact I slept pretty well.

In the morning, we continued to chat over a long breakfast, and she bemoaned the enormous amount of clearing up which follows a death. She hadn't realised, she joked, as this was her first experience. In fact, part of her 'clearing up' provoked a change of direction during this period of fieldwork, although it didn't happen until after I had returned home, when I received a gift through the post from Mrs Tamaru. It wasn't a special gift, in that she had probably ordered a large number to send out by way of thanks to all those who had made gifts to her, but it triggered off a line of thinking which turned out to herald a turning point in my approach.

The contents of the package were quite charming – five tiny dishes for individual servings of sauce – but it was the way they were wrapped which drew my attention. To proceed from the parcel which was delivered to my door, I had to remove no fewer than seven layers of packaging to reveal the contents. Some had a clear purpose – protection of the breakable material, paper marked with symbols of death and the afterlife, and an outer covering to transmit the gift through the mail – but there was no functional explanation which could account completely for the seven layers. Anyone who lives in Japan for long notes the attention paid to packaging, and some complain about the apparent waste of resources, but I suddenly became aware of the great potential wrapping has for a subtle form of communication.

In the following weeks I began to pay greater attention to wrapping, and I noticed the use of wrapping materials, such as paper, cloth and straw, in other ways. In reading, and in discussions about the use of language, I discovered a neat connection between the use of polite and formal language and the use of other markers, such as wrapping, to express the same sentiment. The Japanese word for politeness, *teinei*, also means 'care', and care for an object, by the appropriate use of wrapping, expresses care for the person to whom it is presented. A single-page letter may be wrapped in an extra blank sheet to express the same sentiment.

This care is also expressed by the use of language which 'wraps' words in a form appropriate for a particular occasion. Verbal 'wrapping' might lend formality to a special occasion such as a wedding or a funeral. It might make more palatable the communicating of a difficult decision, or an expression of discontent. Language might also 'wrap' a group of people and distinguish them from others, and, where the principle is used intentionally, it may create an image a person wishes to present to the outside world. Clothes contribute to this image, of course, and the headmaster had noted a parallel between the clothes used by the upper classes in England and those used on a ritual occasion. It was interesting, then, to hear that the most formal kimono, worn in the ancient court and by a bride at imperial weddings, has no fewer than twelve layers. Here was food for thought indeed.

Some of the most insightful moments of a period of anthropological fieldwork emerge through shocks and disasters. They inevitably provoke a valuable kind of spontaneous reaction in informants, and, sometimes, a fairly crude kick-start to thought processes turning over in no particularly systematic direction in the ethnographer. The discovery of the family background of my son's close friend was really only the confirmation of a suspicion, and while it held some exciting possibilities, it was not, at that moment, an earth-shattering revelation for the research. When the father of a boy in Callum's class committed suicide, I learned about the differential dissemination of knowledge. However, the death of the father of one of my oldest friends in Japan provoked a moment of real insight.

Chapter 11

Paper walls and flowers at the bank

Some observations begin to confirm the new insight, but a low period for the anthropologist indicates that feelings are not always related to the seriousness of the problem during fieldwork.

Musings on the implications of the multi-layered gift, and other possible parallels, led to an alteration in the focus of my research. It was not immediate, nor, for a very long time, clearly formed, but I began to reexamine other examples of layering for their potential for a kind of communication of which I had not previously been aware. I also began to notice other forms of wrapping, and the way these could sometimes be related to the use of language. Takako was helpful on this front because she was familiar with some of my reading, and she could quickly find relevant references, such as the example mentioned in the previous chapter of wrapping a single-page letter in an extra blank sheet.

Another line of thought was inspired one morning in Takako's house when I found her busy with a man stripping the covers of her cupboards. These were floor-to-ceiling affairs, exactly like those in our own house, which enclosed and concealed a capacious storage space, accessed through large, sliding doors. The same sliding doors are used to partition rooms in a traditional Japanese house, and they can be removed to open up a larger area for family gatherings and other special events. Like the latticed window frames, which filter bright sunshine and create a pleasant, subdued light, they are covered in a stiff form of paper which can be renewed as they become dirty or damaged. Replacing this paper is thus part of a redecorating process.

The sliding doors are called *fusuma,* and the man who was here to recover them is called a *fusuma-ya,* a skilled occupation which he explained required many years of training. Very often an art such as this is passed down through the generations in a natural family line, but his own father had been a *geta-ya*, making the slip-on wooden footwear which has little stilts to lift the feet off the ground in wet weather, and there was less demand for these now that the streets are better paved and drained. He had therefore decided to take up another occupational craft, had attended university to study the subject, and then become an apprentice to learn the skills. He said that it had taken him about ten years to achieve competence.

Fusuma are by no means just functional, and they very often depict a delicate mountain scene, repeated on each door throughout the room. In some palaces and temples open to the public, the work of a famous artist is permanently on display on the *fusuma*, and may be a special feature of the location. The opening and closing of doors in a large area may also create a series of layers. These sliding doors, then, offer a way to create, and re-create, the living environment, and to adjust it to changing tastes. Takako explained that she had chosen a plain colour for her cupboard doors, for this seemed to be the current preference in Tokyo, the city local people look to for their lead in fashion. It was a colour very close to white, with a visible grain.

Plain white paper is also used for the wrapping of a formal gift, and its quality is measured in its texture, and in the visible grain. It is also used to wrap money when this is presented, and, in both cases, further details, such as the colour of the string, indicate whether the occasion is a celebratory one or a sad one, such as a funeral or a memorial. The pile of envelopes I had seen at the Tamaru house were finished with black and white string, for example. The plain white paper indicates the formality, or ritual element, of the gift, but this feature is also used for an expensive, high-class gift. Again, there seemed to be an overlap between ritual and the expression of superiority.

Paper-making is a highly respected art in Japan, and a piece of calligraphy may be admired for the paper used as much as for the script itself. Paper is thus used in each of these three contexts – the *fusuma*, the gifts and the art – as a means of communication, as a means of expressing taste and aesthetic appreciation. Takako had chosen to 'wrap' her cupboard doors, and therefore part of her room, in a type of paper which would demonstrate her awareness of contemporary fashion. Those of her acquaintances who were aware of such niceties would undoubtedly be those for whom she reserved her use of Tokyo language, and this was another subtle way of expressing a kind of class allegiance. It led me to think about the significance of the 'wrapping' of space.

Shortly after this, I came across another rather different example of the wrapping of space when I went down to the local bank. This time, the wrapping was temporary, but it was quite remarkable. To take money out of one's account in this branch, it is necessary to enter the main door of the bank, and turn into the 'cash corner'. Here are located the machines which dispense cash, and, usually, nobody employed in the bank becomes involved in the transaction, although an electronic voice sounds a welcome, as a tiny human figure on the screen bows to each customer. On this occasion, however, as I passed through the door, I was greeted by two smartly dressed human bank employees. One bowed deeply as the other presented me with a gift. The whole public area of the bank was decorated with flowers.

It was impossible to ignore these special arrangements, and I enquired immediately about the occasion for such celebration. The employees announced proudly that they had just appointed a new branch manager, a woman in fact, and, shortly thereafter, the new manager came over to introduce herself. What I didn't realise until later, when I read the announcement in the local press, was that the new manager of my branch of the Chiba District Bank was the first woman ever to be appointed as manager of a bank in Japan. The flowers had been used to announce a very special celebration, and I had been lucky enough to witness it. I resolved to seek out this new heroine for an interview, and she later proved to be a very useful friend.

In fact, the bank at which I held my account in Japan provided me, usually by chance, with quite a few insights into Japanese ways of doing things. I had first opened an account at this bank during my last stay, when I lived nearer to another local branch. They had never had the experience of looking after a foreign customer there before, and we learned some of the procedures together. It was a small branch, where I usually saw the same clerk, a Mrs Ohkawa, and she took a personal interest in my situation. First of all, it was necessary to acquire a personal seal, since a signature is not considered sufficient security for identification, so I went off to have one made.

A seal depicts the owner's name, written in their chosen *kanji*, or Chinese characters, for a Japanese customer, but foreigners are usually encouraged to write their names in a phonetic, cursive script known as *kana*. My name would have required four such characters, which would hardly fit neatly onto the end of the small seal used for bank purposes, so I decided to ask for two characters which could be read as 'Hendori'. This was the nearest pronunciation that could be managed, and I had already chosen two characters, in consultation with Japanese friends, when I first lived in Japan. The literal meaning of these two characters is 'strange bird', which had seemed very appropriate when I chose them, for 'bird' was at the time popular colloquial English for 'girl', and 'strange' is, of course, the adjective used for foreigners who try to behave like Japanese.

My friends had laughed at the time, and I had yet to discover that the same character for *hen*, or 'strange', is used for the slang use of 'different', to refer to the mentally ill. Indeed, it was not until I returned to the bank, proudly bearing my new seal, that the full force of this slang expression was brought home to me. Ohkawa-*san* had paled visibly. 'This is not really a very nice way to write your name', she had explained patiently, 'this use of *hen* has a derogatory meaning, you know.' I had retorted that I knew the way it was used to describe foreigners, and I didn't mind, and I told her about the slang use of 'bird' in English, now a little less appropriate since I had married and given birth to two children.

She had not been easily convinced, feeling perhaps that proper respect could not be given to a customer who chose such a literally strange name, and she had explained the slang use of 'different' as well. What she had not explained, though her attitude was an element in my own learning about the matter, was the importance people attach to their names. I knew that some people change their names, or the characters for them, on marriage for example, as I had come across examples of this previously, but I was only beginning to get a feel for the effect an apparently inauspicious use of characters could invoke. My seal had been quite expensive, however, and it had taken a couple of days to make, so I was loath to delay further the opening of my account.

As it turned out, the use of these characters for my name proved to be quite auspicious. Ohkawa-*san* had not only dealt with my business throughout our previous stay, offering a regular opportunity to chat about our respective families and other items of everyday life, but she also happened to be on duty at the Toyama branch when I turned up to open a new account on this present visit. Although five years had passed, she had no trouble at all remembering my name, and we took up our relationship where it had left off. She had been transferred to the town branch during our absence, part of a company routine to move their employees between different positions. Unfortunately, however, the reshuffle which brought the first female branch manager to this branch also sent Mrs Ohkawa to a more distant one.

On the day I enquired about interviewing the new branch manager, whose name was Matsushita, she was not available. I left a message with her deputy, who said that he had heard about me from Ohkawa-san, and he promised to pass on my enquiry. Before Matsushita-san phoned back, however, there was a call from Mrs Ohkawa, who suggested we meet again before I returned to England. My return was still some time off, but I followed up her suggestion, and found out that reactions to the new appointment were not universally positive. Some approved, she said, but others felt that Matsushita-san had just been appointed to pay lip service to the new Equal Opportunities Law. Others, perhaps herself, though she didn't mention it, had been passed over for this piece of political correctness (these were not the words she used, but the sentiment was there!).

Actually Mrs Ohkawa might have been getting a little disgruntled with the bank anyway, for she had given up her job by the time I returned again a few years later, and was running a bar. She said it was because her husband, who had worked in the same bank, had been ill and had had to leave. On an earlier occasion she had confided that life was pretty stringent at the bank. Although staff were entitled to forty days' leave a year, no one took more than three, except for public holidays, because none of them wanted to rock the boat. If they did such a thing they would surely be passed over for promotion, she had said. I suppose if people engage in such self-denial in order to succeed, and then see others promoted over their heads, they may well feel disillusioned. Ohkawa-san seemed happier in her bar.

Matsushita-san's attitude was, understandably, quite different. A woman in her early forties, she was smartly dressed and clearly very bright. When I asked her how she had come to achieve her distinction, she explained that she had won several competitions within the bank, even being awarded two holidays in Hawaii at the bank's expense. She was particularly good at persuading customers to reinvest their 'spare' money, it seems, and I remembered ruefully turning down Ohkawa's suggestion that I move some of my money to a savings account. In fact I never had enough 'spare' to make it worthwhile, but I noticed an interesting system which came into play when I had money to deposit, and a small 'thank-you gift' was produced. My grant was only enough for paper hankies, I think, but those with larger sums received better gifts.

This system may or may not have been introduced by Matsushita-san,

I never followed it up, but what I did discover was that my own friend, Takako, had withdrawn her money from this particular bank because she felt that Matsushita had been too pushy. However, Takako had been impressed that she remembered her name after meeting her only once. Many people must have been even further impressed, because Matsushita had clearly done very well. I kept an account at this branch after I left, and when I returned, some eight years on, she had been promoted even further, into the higher echelons of head office in Chiba. She still remembered my name even then, and helped me out of a situation that the local branch couldn't handle.

My interview with Matsushita also helped me to understand bank language, and attitudes towards the customers. I had noticed a fairly high level of politeness in the bank, and she explained that although they are not specially trained in the use of language, they are expected to treat the customer, who is referred to as a 'guest', with great respect. Thus phrases are chosen which put the bank employee in a deferential position. Bank employees are partly chosen for their ability to speak politely, she explained, and they also practise dealing with different kinds of people, such as those with a short temper, or who find bank matters difficult to understand. I had found myself in both situations during my stay and, I have to admit, the staff were very diplomatic.

Banking business seemed always to take an interminably long time, from my point of view, and it was inevitable that one be asked to sit down and wait. Grants arriving from England were an especially unusual occurrence in this bank, but all the customers seemed to have to follow the same procedure. While waiting, I used to observe, and I absorbed, though only later properly analysed, another example of the wrapping of space, or possibly people. This one was similar to the situation in the school staff-room, where higher-ranking employees were seated further away from public access than the lower ones. In the bank, too, the smiling faces behind the counter were the least exalted employees, and promotion moved an individual back through the open office. The manager, like the headmaster, had an enclosed area at the very back.

In fact this is fairly standard for office arrangements in Japan, and as one proceeds up the hierarchy, one is likely to spend less time dealing with sundry enquiries, and more with one's own specific business. Matsushita-*san* stressed that language use between employees of different ranks is strictly observed, thereby reflecting these spatial arrangements, but she also noted that the general level of politeness drops once the door for the customers is locked, and things are much more relaxed during recreation. Clearly the image presented to the outside world is very important in a bank, and this is again reflected in the use of uniforms for the employees immediately in contact with the customers. These are standard throughout the different branches, and the same image is reproduced for the electronic bowing figure in the cash machine.

Matsushita-*san* was quite firm about the use of language, especially amongst her employees, to whom she seemed quite curt, and I asked her whether she felt the need to be assertive, perhaps more masculine, as a woman in an unusually high-ranking position. She confirmed that she spoke more loudly than other women in the bank, and in a lively, slightly rough fashion more characteristic of men. Takako Doi had recently been appointed as leader of the Japan Socialist Party, and my own friend Takako had noted that Doi's language had been very masculine as she rose through the ranks, but that since she had been appointed leader, she had become more feminine. Matsushita had noticed this too, and she recognised the value of such a technique, though she could not be quite as rough in a bank.

There was a personal quality to my relationship with Matsushita-*san*, however, and I am still confused about the way this was manifested in banking practice. She gave me time for an interview, and I helped her son with his English pronunciation. We exchanged a gift or two, as one is wont to do to confirm a social link, but whether any customer would have received the treatment I am about to describe, I cannot possibly say. To make each customer feel personally cared for is undoubtedly a laudable goal in any business, and it was specifically related to the use of language in some of the books I had read. It certainly worked for me with Matsushita-*san*, but I would need another trip and another focus to place this event completely in a Japanese context.

The situation arose because of a delay in the arrival of my grant from England, and this created an awkward cash-flow problem. First, it had made me late with paying the rent, and on the day that the money arrived, a Monday, I went along to withdraw enough to settle this debt. The machine refused to cooperate so I was forced to enquire at the counter. It appeared that some kind of bank rule had come into force, and although the money had arrived, I would not be allowed to use it until Wednesday. I explained the situation at the hospital office, and went to work at my desk. Shortly afterwards the telephone rang, and Matsushita-*san* was there, offering to lend me some money. 'I don't have much,' she said, 'but if it would help ...'.

Clearly this would have been a personal loan, and I turned down her kind offer, as politely as I could, wondering why they didn't simply offer me an overdraft. When I returned to the bank on the Wednesday, I noticed that a sum of 10,000 yen had indeed been paid into my account, and that the school lunch money had been withdrawn, an automatic transaction which I could not otherwise have paid. Matsushita-*san* had stepped in, it seemed, and saved the day. I paid her back, personally, with a 10,000 yen note, but, for some inexplicable reason, it made me feel very low. This was the day when I felt most like a strange foreigner, getting special treatment.

Part III

The role of experts

Chapter 12

A foreigner at the 'Culture Festival'

Participation in cultural activities opens up some new ideas: Does relaxation come with a true mastery of the art of the tea ceremony? And is language affected by the wearing of a kimono?

Low periods do occur during fieldwork, and they tend to coincide with an awareness of a great gulf in knowledge, or a general feeling of alienation from the lives of those around. I suppose that, following the 'high' of a moment of insight, it was only to be expected that a low would follow, but the incident in the bank was hardly momentous, and it was probably intended as a friendly act. With children in tow, there are more ups and downs, as each of them runs through similar experiences grappling with life in a foreign culture. As I thought on the bank incident, I recalled an earlier low, involving Hamish, and I realised that again it concerned the concepts of borrowing and lending.

He had come home one day in something of a fluster, and flung down a note from the teacher, this time on a piece of paper, rather than in his notebook. The teacher's tone was exasperated, and it recounted a series of incidents that day during which she said Hamish had failed to cooperate with the other pupils. She asked me to speak to him, but it was a short sentence at the end that I found most disturbing: 'Could you please be careful that Hamish is not bringing home objects borrowed from friends in the class.' Now, Hamish has his faults, like any child, but dishonesty was not one of them, and I decided to investigate this implied accusation further. I accompanied Hamish to school the following morning.

Mrs Takagi was an energetic young woman who took her role seriously, and I had several conversations with her over the period. She set the children to a task and came out of the classroom to tell me about

the incident which had prompted her to write in such a way. Hamish
followed. Apparently he had borrowed a pencil from a girl in the class,
and it had got broken. Hearing this, Hamish raced back into the classroom and offered the same girl 50 yen to buy a new one. She then
came out too and I explained what it was for. She refused it, saying
that she had plenty of pencils at home. I suggested that she buy some
sweets. She had plenty of those too, she said. Finally, Hamish said he
was sorry, in his best Japanese, the two shook hands and the girl
returned to her work.

Mrs Takagi explained that the girl had not minded lending the
pencil, indeed children passed these things around amongst themselves
all the time, but she had been upset that it was not returned in the
condition in which she had lent it. I appreciated her concern, and
commented that Hamish had not yet had to take his own pens and
pencils to school in England, where the school provided them, so he
had still to learn this lesson – I wondered, in fact, whether it was
precisely to avoid incidents of this sort that the English system had
evolved. I remembered my granny quoting the words of Polonius from
Hamlet, 'Neither a borrower nor a lender be', and I suggested that I tell
Hamish to avoid borrowing things from his classmates.

This seemed to upset the teacher even further, however, and she
asked him merely to be careful. It was a good way for children to share
their possessions, she explained, and they enjoyed finding new pieces
of equipment to show, and lend, to their friends. Stationery shops in
Japan are full of exciting objects, as we had already noticed, and this
system of exchange seemed to be an important part of school life, an
opportunity to learn to value the objects of others. If Hamish refused to
take part, it would cut him off from this lesson, as well as from significant communication with his classmates.

As I thought on this conversation later, I also recalled the idea
that wrapping a gift demonstrates care for the object inside and therefore care for the recipient. Care for a borrowed object, and its return
in pristine condition, may also express care for the owner, and the
little girl could have felt offended less about her pencil than about
the opinion Hamish apparently expressed towards her by damaging
her pencil. I doubted that he had meant such an insult as clearly as
she took it, and I didn't even think that far at the time, but I had
understood that objects were being used to teach important lessons
about social relationships and mutual respect in Japan, even in the
classroom. I was glad that I had taken the trouble to visit Mrs Takagi
and work things out.

We had not even reached the reason why she thought he might be bringing things home, and we had learned a useful lesson. In fact, the former turned out to be a mistaken assumption involving another teacher who had seen Hamish run outside – without his shoes – clutching some objects. This incident was soon resolved too, and Hamish was reminded about the distinction between inside and outside space. As it happened, the headmaster heard about the events of the day, and he called us in. He smiled broadly, and told me not to worry. Hamish is bound to be naughty sometimes because he doesn't understand everything yet, he said, and he will get bored. He had decided to ask a teacher to come in once a week to give the boys some lessons in English.

I was impressed, and I thanked him profusely. He was evidently concerned to do his best to help these foreign children feel at home. Hamish was with us as we spoke, and the head kept picking up things on his desk and giving them to Hamish – first, a diary, then a small Japanese dictionary, then a set of crayons. Hamish was pleased, of course, but I began to feel uneasy. Were these to keep, I wondered? The head reassured me that they were, but I was concerned about the implications since gifts are very closely related to their obligations in Japan. It was not possible to press him further, and Hamish did settle down, so perhaps it was much simpler than I had thought. If the school, represented by the head, gave him gifts, he would behave better in return. What a wonderful way to use a few objects.

From the time that I joined my *ikebana* (flower-arranging) class, which later came also to involve a class in tea ceremony, I found the intense concentration on aesthetic pursuits immensely therapeutic. However stressed or depressed I might have felt as I cycled off to my class, however lively the children, I would usually return in a calmer frame of mind. The teacher's attention to detail in the way she prepared for us, and taught us, made the whole experience of being in her house a pleasant one. The study itself sometimes seemed a little tedious at first, with very small adjustments to the length and angle of the plants apparently being of great importance in *ikebana* (see Figure 3), and minute movements of the body absorbing all one's concentration in the tea ceremony, but the end result was edifying.

In fact all this is part of the training in the artistic pursuits I had chosen, and the same principles apply to other Japanese arts, but the attention to the surroundings of the rooms and the garden were now fitting my new line of thinking on the wrapping of space. A tea master (or mistress) is expected to spend a great deal of time preparing the

Figure 3 The flower-arranging class

space visitors will use, and this is also considered to be a means of communicating care for them. The garden should be neat and freshly watered, but possibly with an artistic shower of newly fallen leaves, or petals, as a special touch. The tea room should be pristine, with a suitable scroll hanging in a special alcove called a *tokonoma*, and an arrangement of *ikebana* placed beneath it. The tea utensils and cakes are carefully chosen and add to the overall aesthetic experience.

In November, my teacher asked me if I would participate in the town's 'Culture Festival'. We would together create a sample of *ikebana*, to be displayed under my name, and there would be an opportunity to examine a great number of other arrangements from different traditions. We would also have a chance to take tea with a famous tea master. The event was to be held in a large cultural centre which would house exhibitions of all kinds of other works of art and study. I agreed, and we made arrangements to go there as a class. The previous day we would meet at the centre to put together our various contributions.

The teacher provided all the materials for my entry. It was to be created around a pair of shiny roof tiles of a dark aquamarine colour, with water concealed underneath, the flowers and branches arranged so that they appeared to be growing out of or, in the case of the flowers, having fallen upon this fragment of roof. She showed me exactly how to fix the living materials in place, and I simply followed her example. When I had finished, she rearranged things slightly, and sent me on my way. On the next day, when we returned, she had even altered it again, adding a new branch at the back, though my name was still clearly displayed. The important thing, I suppose, was that it appeared on her table, along with the contributions of her other pupils.

Other teachers with entries in the festival were operating in much the same way, closely overseeing the work of their pupils, and a great number of splendid arrangements were assembled. Again, the attention to detail was very noticeable, and while I was standing around, I was set to polish the leaves of the entry of one of my fellow-pupils. I was struck by the enormous effort which is put into these often very simple-seeming creations, and how, in the end, they create a very natural look. A nook or cranny from the natural world (as it were) is re-created through much time and careful cutting and crafting, so that the highest aim of the cultural elaboration of the plants is to put them back into an arrangement as near as possible to a natural one.

This objective is different, it seemed to me, from the way we arrange flowers in Britain, where the end result is very definitely cultural, though still aiming to be aesthetically pleasing. I was shocked to discover that a Japanese friend of a friend had returned from only six months in London to set up as a teacher of Western flower 'arrange-ment', whereas in Japan it takes years to become qualified to teach *ikebana*. The creation of the cultural version of the natural is highly prized in the preparation of food in Japan, too, where slices of raw fish may even be returned to the still twitching body they were cut from, to be served at the table, and living prawns may be thrown to the hotplate before the customers' eyes. The preparation of food is of course also an artistic pursuit.

When I arrived at the 'Culture Festival' itself, I found that my teacher and some of my classmates were wearing kimonos for the occa-sion, which added an extra dimension to the aesthetic quality of the activities. It was a pleasant, sunny day, and a corner had been arranged outside for the ceremonial serving of tea. There was a raised platform, with a red-and-white backcloth, where the utensils were displayed, and a large umbrella in the same hues provided an area of shaded seating. As we approached, we met some other local members of tea ceremony circles, also clad in kimonos, and during the introductions I noticed that the language used amongst them was of a formal quality which added again to the aesthetics of the occasion.

It was not hugely deferential. Indeed, the exchanges were expressing mutual respect, with subtle indicators of relative status, but the level of *keigo* chosen simply raised the tone of the occasion. In strict linguistic terms they were using a kind of language which may be called 'polite' (*teineigo*), in the same sense as its use meaning 'care', but some linguists call this form 'beautification language' (*bikago*). At various levels, then, my companions were drawing upon the resources available to them to create a cultural experience beyond the entries on display inside. I wondered whether these women always chose these forms of greeting, or whether they raised the level of their speech when they dressed in kimonos.

Some linguists criticise women for using too much *bikago*, suggesting they compete to outshine one another, and a Japanese text-book gives an example in which half a page of female language about a garden is shown to be parallel to a couple of lines when men exchange the same compliments. The women may use language to put one another down, they may also compete in their use of kimonos, and, in the case of my teacher, by adding a foreign name to their *ikebana* entries, but the language used here was also quite appropriate to the occasion. It wrapped the greetings in a harmonious form of words which fitted perfectly the elegant wrapping of the figures of the speakers as we all approached a corner of space which had also been literally 'wrapped' for the tea ceremony.

The fresh-air version of the tea ceremony is relatively informal, in fact, and allows a fairly large number of people, unschooled like myself, to come along and participate. Two women were carrying out the procedure for a couple of principal guests seated in front of them, and the rest of us were served by younger girls. First, we were brought an exquisite little cake, which we placed on a piece of white paper my teacher skilfully produced at just the right moment. When we had eaten that, we were brought our tea, in a bowl, which we consumed without further ado. This was a kind of trial run for me, for my teacher was also determined to take me into the more formal ceremony being held inside. She was doing quite a good job of persuading me to add 'tea classes' to my *ikebana* practice.

We wandered in fairly slowly, passing through the *ikebana* rooms as we went, and admiring and discussing the final versions of the entries we had seen being put together the previous day. I was asked for my comments and opinions, which I felt most unqualified to make, for my comparisons with British flower arranging did not seem appropriate. More successful for me were the explanations I received from the teachers, and others, about the differences between the various schools of *ikebana*. There were some large, sumptuous examples of a school called Sōgetsu, which were unmistakable in their size and level of display, but the chief quality of the Ikenobo school, which my teacher espoused, is a refined sobriety known in Japanese as *shibui*.

Our admiration and gentle analysis of the display was rather tiringly (for the others) punctuated by the sporadic interruptions of Hamish and Callum, who popped in to see why we were taking so long, and to report on some of the other things they had found. There was a room full of elaborate polished roots, for example, another with decorative stones, and a third with bonsai. One of our neighbours was involved with collections of stamps. He had invited us round one evening to see his English examples, and since these were pages and pages of pictures of the Queen's head, with only very minute differences between them, we gave the stamp room a wide berth. Rooms with scrolls and other types of painting and calligraphy were more appealing, and this is where Jenny first thought she would like to take up the ink brush-work.

Eventually, we arrived at the inside tea ceremony room, which positively exuded formality. There was a waiting room at one side, where people were seated neatly in line, and young girls in kimonos fluttered nervously in and out. For some reason, our group was pushed through ahead, despite our protests, and we found ourselves next to the *fusuma* sliding door, slightly open to the room beyond, where the ceremony was being held. This was the real thing, and when it came to our turn, my teacher eased herself through on her knees, bowing before and after, placing her fan in front of her as she did so. I tried to follow suit, but she told me to stand up, so I walked through as neatly as I could manage.

We sat ourselves in a tidy row, kneeling back on our feet in the proper fashion, and the officiator, a man this time, came out from an inner room and greeted us with a deep, low bow. He was also wearing a kimono, but he didn't serve the tea, although he was clearly in charge, answering the polite, conventional enquiries about the scroll and the bowls used for the thick green tea. This time much more attention was paid to the procedure, and the movements we made were prescribed and, where necessary, prompted by our teacher. It would have been an advantage to be wearing a kimono at this stage, I felt, because one's position would already be constrained into the appropriate shape, with no pleats or frills flapping uncontrolled around the knees.

Most of the people present were pupils of the tea ceremony, and most of them seemed nervous and tense about getting things right. Even our teacher was on her best behaviour in front of this grand man, who was evidently superior in the hierarchy. The master himself, on the other hand, seemed quite relaxed, and I supposed that when one reaches a certain stage of training things become so much second nature that one no longer needs to worry. In fact, I was probably still oversimplifying things, for this basic ceremony of the making, pouring and imbibing of a cup of tea seems to represent the epitome of esoteric understanding in a Japanese view.

When we got home I asked Takako whether people change their language according to what they are wearing, and she did not answer immediately. She visualised herself in a kimono and tried to imagine speaking. She couldn't separate the circumstances of the dress from the dress itself, suggesting that an occasion for a kimono would probably demand polite language anyway, but she did point out that one could hardly kick up one's legs and jump about in a kimono. This was precisely what we did at tennis, of course, when we were very informal, and we could do it because we were wearing skimpy dresses. This was certainly worth thinking about, and I resolved to observe dress and language in future, along with situation and relative status.

Chapter 13

'Your Japanese is psychological torture'

Some interesting insights offered by a Japanese anthropologist; a professor of linguistics seems to be less than helpful, though this may just be the sensitivity of the researcher feeling out of her depth.

Throughout our stay in Toyama I made several visits to Tokyo, only two hours away by train, to see Yoko, the research assistant I had recruited in Oxford, and to call in at the university to which I was officially attached as a visiting researcher. There was often a seminar to attend, and I could use the library and meet Andrew, another Oxford anthropologist who was also visiting Keio University. It gave me an opportunity to stand back a little from life 'in the field', to observe and discuss the much more complex interaction of the big city, and to analyse my findings (and his) with a fellow-European. Andrew had previously worked in Bali, and his comparisons between Japanese and Balinese systems of thought were sometimes very revealing.

He had, for example, noted some interesting parallels in the use of concentric circles in the ordering of people and space in Bali and Japan, and these helped me in thinking about the layering of the various forms of wrapping I was observing. In Japan, there is a definite correlation between the language used with other people and their proximity in social terms, and a Japanese scholar whose work Andrew had been reading had suggested that each Japanese is surrounded by layers of people of diminishing proximity in a series of such circles. Thus the family forms the closest such group, then perhaps the neighbourhood, the school, the workplace, the town, and so forth.

In practice, things are never quite so simple, but it is a useful way to think about relationships, and I was encouraged to learn that children in primary school actually learn about their social world in a way which reproduces the model. During one of my chats with the head-master, he had explained that they focus on the family in the first year, the neighbourhood in the second, the town or city in the third, the prefecture in the fourth, the nation in the fifth, and the rest of the world in the sixth year. Implications of this idea were not immediate or all-embracing, but it did occasionally help to explain or elucidate something which had previously seemed elusive. Some of my informants also illustrated the pattern in various ways.

The train to Tokyo was used frequently by members of my circles of acquaintance in Toyama, for example, so I met several people by chance during the journeys. One of the housewives' group had commented that you can't relax and let your hair down until you arrive at Tokyo Station because you never know who might see you on the way. The arrival was like a kind of release for her, for she could lose herself in the crowds, and escape, albeit temporarily, the constraints of community life. These can be quite stringent in a provincial town, and Takako had once described to me graphically her fear of being ostracised by her *nakama*, a fate she anticipated would be brought about by insufficient attention to the formalities of social life. Tokyo provided an escape to a layer of life where these were freer.

Yoko's perspective on life was a little different, for she had trained as an anthropologist, and was now working freelance for a company which was specifically concerned with language and image. She was also married, but yet to have children, so her time was still much more her own to use as she would. In Oxford we had drawn up various plans for the project, and Yoko had agreed to act as a kind of mole, working in a complex part of Japanese society, and quietly making observations of the language used by her associates. Her findings were invaluable, and she made some very helpful comments on my own work as it proceeded. Yoko also helped me to locate appropriate books for the research, and she saved me hours by skimming various texts for useful material.

One book to which Yoko directed me was a wonderfully sardonic analysis of what she referred to as 'middle-class consciousness'. With the title of *Kinkonkan*, it wasn't an academic text, but a joint work by a cartoonist and a journalist, setting out and illustrating a system of clas-sifying people by their resources and the way they display them. The obvious markers are, of course, houses, cars and clothes, but this book revealed many more possibilities, perhaps best summarised in English as demonstrations of 'taste'. This could literally be food preferences, notably those Western items which were currently fashionable, but it also included the use of language, spoken and unspoken, and material indicators such as the choice of wrapping paper in which to present gifts. This book gave me many ideas for the observation of other forms of 'wrapping', and Takako's estimation of plain white for the current Tokyo fashion in *fusuma* was confirmed within its pages.

Yoko's approach was flexible enough to allow her to move, with me, from the strict focus on *keigo* to casting about more widely for examples of wrapping. She spoke on one occasion about her own pleasure in shopping in a department store where she was treated deferentially, and she pointed out that the treatment includes greetings by uniformed employees at the doors, the provision of a lift operator, again uniformed, to recite the contents of the various floors, and the attractive and pleasing surroundings in which to browse. The uniformed employees use very formal and stylised language, and Yoko suggested that there is a measure of protection involved. A young girl alone in a lift could be vulnerable, for example, but her uniform, white gloves and machine-like voice make it difficult for customers to take advantage.

The big department stores are prestigious places to shop, and they all have very clearly marked carrier bags so that those who make purchases can indicate their source, especially in the presentation of gifts. Most stores in Japan will wrap gifts as a matter of course, but Yoko pointed out that the larger department stores have 'wrapping corners' where a customer can pay to have a different sort of paper, and this extra degree of choice allows for further communication. Paper may be chosen for some special personal reason, or it may be chosen to indicate social status, or a respect for tradition. One of Yoko's acquaintances, apparently from a family with very high-class credentials, spurned all manufactured paper and recycled her own in a paper-making machine.

This kind of inverse snobbery, which also indicated a caring concern for the environment, requires considerable self-confidence. In *Kinkonkan*, Yoko's recommended book, members of the Japanese middle class were distinguished according to various sub-groups, and a relatively large group were heavily committed to buying brand-name clothes to demonstrate their wealth. A smaller, but superior, group wear things passed down to them by their grandmothers – a neat way of suggesting generations of good taste, which has an edge over sheer economic advantage, especially in a society which used to rank merchants at the bottom of the social scale. This practice is easily recognisable in Britain, as is the kudos attached in some circles to an emphasis on conservation. In all cases, there are parallels with the use of language.

I actually had a sort of living laboratory in Tokyo to test out some of the ideas Yoko and I had been discussing in the more impersonal spheres of the big city. One good point of comparison for me were the different universities I had occasion to visit. Universities are ranked according to various criteria in Japan, and the two professors who were kind enough to help me formally with my academic pursuits were attached to three between them. One of these was Tokyo University, the most highly ranked in the public sector according to academic criteria, the others were Keio, a highly ranked private establishment, and Seishin Joshi, a women's university which was renowned for the calibre of the families who chose it for their daughters as much as for its academic credentials.

The students at each of these universities use language which marks them in distinctive ways, and the invitations which I received to attend seminars allowed me also to observe this interesting social factor. The girls of Seishin Joshi were very skilled in the use of the polite *teineigo*, for example, whereas the female members of the Keio anthropology class used a more brusque form of language which differed little from that of their male counterparts. The most striking difference was evident in the visits sometimes made after the seminars to a nearby hostelry, a practice much more common amongst the students at Tokyo and Keio universities than at the more genteel Seishin. One student from Seishin who was present at such a gathering at Keio one evening clearly felt quite uncomfortable.

On one particular visit to Tokyo, I was invited by the professor at Keio, Professor Suzuki, an eminent and rather famous linguist, to attend a weekly seminar he was running on the subject of English as a foreign language. This man had a theory, of which I was aware, about the uniqueness of the Japanese language, and how this made it impossible for foreigners ever to learn it successfully. Although he himself spoke very acceptable English, he had also suggested that international communication would be much easier if there were a kind of international English which would give native speakers no particular advantage. The subject of the seminar that week was this international English, and Andrew and I had both been invited.

The presentation was made by a student of Professor Suzuki, who described in some detail why this kind of international language would be beneficial, and how it could be created out of the various forms of English in current use. The result was, unsurprisingly, an English which most closely resembled the version used by Japanese speakers. In the discussion which followed, Professor Suzuki asked Andrew and me whether we could understand Japanese English, and we both replied in the affirmative, although this was not always strictly true. It would have seemed ungenerous, however, to follow this student's sometimes quite laborious English presentation with an admission that everything had not been crystal clear.

Our politeness was not reciprocated, however, for Professor Suzuki followed our expression of support with a comment which seemed to me to be quite stunningly rude. He said that our reaction was interesting because, for him, listening to foreigners speaking Japanese was like a kind of psychological torture. He went on to elaborate: however good their grammar, however perfect their pronunciation, with a foreigner speaking he was never sure of the real intent behind their words. This comment, alone, would have been merely interesting, but Professor Suzuki and I often spoke in Japanese, and he knew perfectly well that I was engaged in a study of the way words, in Japanese, serve to express aspects of this so-called 'real intent'.

The rest of the seminar was lost on me, for I spent the time wondering just how personal he had meant his comment to be. It was said to me, but it was after all said in front of a class of students, and I tried to put myself in his place and imagine what pedagogical message it could have been meant to convey. I wondered if he assumed that because he was speaking in English, he could say something as direct as this without expecting me to extrapolate to my own situation. Reluctantly, because I thought I had got on rather well with him until that moment, I kept on returning to the conclusion that his comment had somehow been a deep and wounding criticism of my ability to carry out the research project on which I was engaged.

It was, of course, never possible to establish exactly his true intention, and this was perhaps the message he had hoped to convey, but afterwards in the bar, fortified by a drink or two, I pressed him a little further on the subject of indirect communication in Japanese. I asked him, for example, about how he himself manipulated this language which he seemed to think so versatile, and he immediately denied that he manipulated language at all. His wife, on the other hand, was a mistress of the art, it seemed, and he gave me some quite concrete examples from his own experience.

In fact his examples could have been taken from the life of a couple in any culture: when she is angry, she will prepare his supper perfectly, but then leave him to it; if he complains about the lack of a clean shirt, she might the next morning prepare twelve. He did note that the Simenon character Maigret and his wife practised some similar forms of indirect communication: she creeping out of the bedroom trying not to disturb him; he, in turn, pretending to be asleep so that she won't realise she has failed – but this behaviour Suzuki interpreted as 'like Japanese'. It was useless trying to convince the professor that other languages have the same possibilities for indirect communication that Japanese does, and I went off back to spend the night at Yoko's place, considerably subdued.

It was clearly another example of the basic lack of an appropriate way to classify the strange breed of foreigner who tries to become conversant with Japanese, but I was surprised that a professor of linguistics should display what I had rather thought simply to be an expression, sometimes found also in Britain, of a lack of experience by an island people who had little contact with outsiders. It was also a sort of arrogance, of course, and Suzuki is certainly not the only Japanese professor to speak, and write, of the unique qualities of Japan and its people. There are parallel works written by psychologists, neurologists and many others. I had just not come into quite such close contact with them.

Yoko was interested in what I had to report. She had spent long enough in England to understand something of my feelings, but she could also explain further a prevalent Japanese point of view. Her comments were in keeping with those Minoru had made when I suggested the parallel between foreigners and the mentally ill. Japanese are becoming uneasy with foreigners now that so many speak Japanese well, she said. They can no longer be treated as 'little', she suggested, and explained that as long as foreigners made mistakes in Japanese they could be regarded as children, less than a 'complete social person', a common phrase used to express the process of converting a child into a fully trained adult.

Some weeks later, Professor Suzuki invited me to address the annual meeting of the Institute of Language and Culture, and I prepared a lecture on the original subject of my research, namely *keigo*, but qualified the title to include the phrase 'from a British perspective'. I explained meticulously how each of the characteristics of *keigo* that I had observed had its counterpart in British English, and, at the end, several members of the audience came to add interesting examples from their own areas of linguistic expertise – Samoan and Hindi being amongst them. I was encouraged that there were at least some Japanese linguists who were open to a more comparative approach, and that they seemed to treat me like an adult, even in Japanese. But then perhaps I had been too sensitive. Professor Suzuki had, after all, invited me to give the lecture.

Chapter 14

A volcanic eruption

The authority of the experts is enough to calm the fears of the anthropologist's Japanese neighbours, but not her family.

As anthropological experiences go, Japan is a relatively comfortable place to do fieldwork. There is little unexplored terrain, there are few dangerous animals, and life-threatening diseases are controlled and usually treatable. Japanese people are mostly kind and extremely helpful, they have an abundance of statistical records, and the language is well documented, even if it does inspire certain prejudices in its native experts. The country does, however, lie along a major geological fault line, and it is prone to suffer from the effects of unpredictable subterranean activity. This factor makes for some spectacular smoking scenery, as well as extraordinary hot springs and bubbling pools. It can also invoke an incredible and unexpected primeval fear.

Our encounter with seismic activity was in fact only rather peripheral, and the event was hardly reported in the international press, but for us it was frightening, though fascinating at the same time. It all started at around tea-time one afternoon in late November. The children were at their swimming class, and Jenny and I were at home, when we noticed that the house had started a gentle kind of shaking. The wooden framework of Japanese houses allows considerable movement, and this was only rather mild, but it was persistent, and it showed no sign of abating. The shutters, which were made of metal, and slid loosely along a set of tramlines, were quivering quite noisily.

We had neighbours upstairs, and, at first, we thought they must be engaging in some kind of strenuous, rhythmic activity, but when we looked out of the door, we noticed that the shutters on our neighbours' house were also shuddering visibly. Furthermore, we could hear a kind of low rumbling noise. Now, I had already experienced several earth-quakes, in Japan and elsewhere, but these strange phenomena were new to me. I went outside to have a look around. There I met several of the neighbours doing the same. Honma-*san*, the mother of the two girls across the road, came out with her daughters, and a bag already packed, looking quite frightened. 'Is it an earthquake?' she asked, 'or what?'

At that moment her mother-in-law popped her head out of the window to call out an answer. 'It's the volcano,' she said, 'they said so on the television.' I had not even been aware that we had a volcano in the immediate vicinity, so I pressed for a bit more detail. Apparently, the activity was some miles away, across the sea on the island of Oshima, where a mountain by the name of Mihara was beginning to erupt. The danger to ourselves was that this might cause related earth-quakes, or possibly a tidal wave. Takako appeared at that moment, racing upstairs to turn off the gas taps, and make things secure. I decided to set off at once to collect the children from swimming, so I grabbed my bike and pulled out into the road.

The journey was quite extraordinary, for the shutters of all the wooden houses on both sides of the road were shuddering gently as I passed, and the deep rumbling noise continued in the distance. As the Shiroyama hill came into view, I noticed a large black cloud gathering behind it, dark and threatening against the palish blue of a late autumnal afternoon. The whole world suddenly seemed strangely insecure. I knew that the volcano was some miles away, but I also knew that new mountains and islands can be thrown up by volcanic activity. I hurried on, as fast as I could cycle, wishing at least to be with my children at such an extraordinary time. I also wanted to share the experience with them.

Inside the pool complex, nothing was different, but people seemed to know what was happening, and some looked quite alarmed. We cycled home, observing the strange phenomena, and as we turned into the area in front of our house the loudspeakers which daily played the first few bars of Beethoven's Fifth Symphony to call children in began to make an announcement. This was an eruption of Mount Mihara, and there was no immediate danger to Toyama residents. Please watch television and listen to the radio, it repeated, two or three times. The television was broadcasting detail about the events, with scientific comment and homely advice, but it was national TV and therefore much more concerned with residents of the island than with those at some distance. As the intensity of the eruption built up, it was decided that these residents should be evacuated to Tokyo.

During the course of the evening, we began to hear loud bangs at irregular intervals, and the house swayed and lurched from time to time. Takako went out to buy some supplies of bread in case there was a serious earthquake, she said, so we followed suit, and also filled our baths and buckets with water in case the the supply got cut off. In our house we packed small emergency bags, with coats, sweaters, passports and the camera, as well as a pack or two of untouchable chocolate. No one else seemed to be doing this, but I thought we should be ready to run up the hill in case there was a tidal wave. We were not at all far above sea level. In the houses of my Japanese neighbours, people were soothed by the reassurance of the television broadcasts which had recently announced that the bangings we could hear were simply displacements of air.

At about 9.45 p.m. we decided to go to bed, in our clothes, to get some sleep in case the night would later be even more disturbed. The house was still shaking and banging, but we did manage to drop off. I woke again at 11, however, rigid with fear and cold. The house was shuddering, and the banging was even more frequent. I went over to Takako's house to find her now quite calm because the television had said there was not much fear of earthquakes. It was showing pictures of the people of Oshima being shipped off the island, some laughing, some quite forlorn. The volcano itself was spectacular, shooting bolts of fire into the air and covered in running molten lava, like a pudding casually decorated with red plum sauce.

Takako said she was going to sleep with the girls, but she was not worried, because the television had reassured her. Honma-*san* said the same in the morning, but quite frankly I found I could not place such faith in these 'experts' who were holding forth. If there was danger of a large earthquake, they would be unlikely to announce it, for mass panic would result, and they could hardly evacuate everyone on the Boso Peninsula. In any case, how did they know? Earthquake predictions had always seemed notoriously inaccurate in my experience, and I had never heard of volcanic ones. Indeed, the Kobe experience a few years later proved my fears quite justified, but there was little to do at that precise moment, so I went back to bed.

The banging continued throughout the night, but I must have dozed off eventually, and the morning broke quiet and sunny. Out in front of the house, everything was covered in a fine layer of deep black volcanic dust. The bicycles, the washing line and each pair of swimming trunks had their own delicate sprinkling, sparkling in the sunshine, so we brought out the camera and recorded the scene for posterity. Takako and Honma-*san* were out admiring this new phenomenon too, and at the corner of the street I found Izuki-*san*, the owner of the 'eel shop', who said he and his family had driven down to the tip of the peninsula to see if they could see the volcano. They had encountered little more than a line of hundreds of cars, their occupants trying to do the same. He quoted an epithet about viewing the fire (or similar disaster) on the other bank – there is little one can do.

At the photographer's shop, where I went to hand in my film, I found that some had been more successful. A couple of people were admiring the results of those who had secured a better view – striking scenes of classic volcanic display. The photographer ran me off a copy of a particularly good example, and we were just filling in my own details on the usual form when the first big earthquake struck. His shop was lined with glass cupboards, which lurched into a spectacular cacophony of motion, but nobody panicked, and he calmly passed me a cushion to hold over my head. His wife appeared at the inner door, with another cushion held over hers, and the two of them estimated that this was quite a severe tremor – probably 3 to 4 on the Japanese scale.

No move was made to leave the shop, however, and after less than a minute it stopped. In the corner, a man on the television had just been discussing the likelihood of a tidal wave in the area, but before I had completed my business an announcement outside reassured the citizens that this was not imminent. I returned home to find that everyone had run out into the street, such was the intensity of the movement, and a man fixing the gas at our place had even pushed Jenny aside in his rush for the door. Shortly afterwards, a TV news bulletin reported that this shock had been particularly bad in Toyama, but felt in Tokyo too, as well as for several hundred miles west and north.

The boys were at school, where, we heard later, they had totally ignored the monthly routine they had practised of donning their earthquake hoods and sitting under their desks. Instead, each from their own classroom, they shot out of the building like bolts of lightning, meeting downstairs in the playground. These foreign boys were clearly not yet properly socialised according to Japanese principles, but then their mother had hardly set them a good example the previous evening. We kept our emergency bags packed for several days.

There were a number of aftershocks, and not a few rumblings. The local loudspeaker kept us in touch with the likelihood of further danger, but there was no opportunity to run off up the hill. At the weekend we received several visitors, from Tokyo and Chiba, and one of my friends declared our house in a particularly vulnerable location.

It wasn't likely to fall, however, for the supple wooden construction is designed to withstand severe shaking. It is apparently buildings which are too rigid which suffer the most damage in an earthquake, and the flexibility of the ground beneath us was also a benefit. This was useful to know, and the visits took our minds off the fear, but it was several nights before we could sleep completely undisturbed.

Meanwhile, the children drew splendid pictures of the volcano in their diaries, and attached little cellophane packets of volcanic dust. The television brought us daily reports of the state of the volcano, the colour of the sea around it, and the fate of the evacuees, accommodated in large halls and schoolrooms in Tokyo and Shizuoka. Stretched out on bedding in tight rows, they seemed remarkably resigned to their lot. For almost a week, only a few brave souls were allowed back to the island to check up on the fate of the animals: pets such as dogs and cats, and a few sorrowful cows.

An interesting programme was constructed around a series of interviews with the dispossessed families, asking them what they had brought with them and what they had thought about as they left their homes. From the point of view of a pair of foreigners with emergency bags at the ready, they seemed totally unprepared. Some had extracted the ancestral tablets from their household Buddhist altars, others had gone for a few clothes, or a change for the baby. One woman had rushed to make rice snacks for her family, and many children had brought their school books. On the whole, there was an air of being taken care of. Like our neighbours, they had put their trust in the authorities, allowing them to determine their fate.

In this case, the families were eventually allowed back to their homes, where they probably found deeper layers of volcanic dust, as well as a new, blacker landscape. The soft, pock-marked stone spewed out of Japan's active volcanos is used to fashion decorative lanterns and other garden ornaments, so there would now be a new supply. The tail of smoke lingered on for the rest of our stay in Japan, and possibly for years thereafter. A new set of hot springs may even have emerged. The event was marked up in the historical records, and we all went about our lives. For us it had been a tremendous experience, something we were unlikely to encounter again, but there was only one small mention of the eruption in our post from home, a single line down the side of a postcard: 'I trust you were nowhere near the volcano which erupted recently in Japan.' We were never able to extract much sympathy from those who were far away. Without the media hype, a disaster may as well not exist....

Chapter 15

Tennis and the 'surreal' dinner

Some apparently informal activities confirm a proposed relationship between language and dress, and demonstrate that even a teacher can be out of depth in an inappropriate context.

Some days after the volcanic eruption, an event took place which allowed me to confirm some of the ideas I had been considering linking language and dress. At the 'Culture Festival' I had observed polite communication between women dressed in kimonos, but I had no opportunity to observe these same women elsewhere. In the tennis class, I had noticed the informality, but I was unsure whether this might have been an idiosyncrasy of our particular teacher. The event in question was a tennis tournament, organised by the PTA of White Lily Kindergarten, so some of the participants were people I had encountered in a variety of other circumstances.

The precise purpose of the event was less than clear, since Mrs Takahashi had never played tennis before and most social activities related to the kindergarten allowed her to shine. At the Bazaar, she had taken pride of place on a stall of exquisite wares, hand-made by mothers of her children; at concerts she positively exuded esoteric knowledge; and at the annual Sports Day, she was resplendent in a crisp white blouse and divided skirt, supervising the events by means of a large loud-hailer. Still, tennis was the sport of the season, and few of her young parents were without some skill and experience, so perhaps it was thought that it might be a good way to raise funds. Tickets were 3,000 yen, to include a picnic lunch.

Members of my own tennis class were also attached to the kindergarten through their children, so we were able to anticipate the event at our meetings. On one occasion, during the drinks after our session, they were running through the names of people who had signed up. Mrs Takahashi was to be present, with her husband, and I noticed that when their names were mentioned, the levels of politeness did rise by a notch or two. It is usual to express respect for people in the choice of levels when speaking about them in the third person, and clearly she and her spouse commanded such respect, though I am not absolutely sure there was not a tinge of irony in the usage. There was mention of her lack of previous experience, so this would have been rather appropriate.

Our tennis group was quite a close one, except for the rather daunting presence of Mrs Obayashi, but elsewhere Takako had explained the need to be careful when speaking about the head of White Lily. During discussions about PTA preparations for the annual Bazaar, when mountains of handiwork are created for sale on behalf of kindergarten funds, she (Takako) had once had the temerity to ask whether no one ever complained about all the work they were expected to do. The committee member present, who was coordinating the activities of a local group, immediately put her in her place: 'Surely no one would do that.' Takako was silenced, but she reported that many people did actually complain. She felt that Mrs T was protected by the committee members from hearing the real opinions of parents.

In general, Takako and other members of the housewives' group were quite careful what they said about whom, and in what company. As I spent time with them I could observe the way language was subtly coded depending on levels of intimacy and shared understanding. One of her closest friends was married into the hospital family, which was one of the oldest and most prestigious in the town, so she was sometimes quite nervous about occasions which involved public appearances together. The annual Bazaar had been one such occasion, and the presence of most of the White Lily parents had made this a particularly sensitive gathering. I wondered whether the tennis tournament would be of the same order.

In the event, the day was quite relaxed. Jenny was a good tennis player, and she had been invited, sometimes with me, to take part in several informal games with the more accomplished players in the town. Some of these were White Lily fathers, so between us we knew most of the people there. One of the best players was in overall charge, aided by our Dr Obayashi and her husband, also a doctor. Mrs Takahashi appeared, sporting shoes and a racket she had purchased the previous day, and the head of the PTA and his wife were also gamely joining in, despite no previous experience. We picked coloured pieces of wool to determine our partners, and I drew the husband of one of our housewives' group for the mixed doubles, and the intrepid Mrs T for the women's.

We started out playing a set each, but this proved too time-consuming, so we eventually settled on reaching four games to win. My male partner and I made it through to the finals, though winning only by a hair's breadth in each game, but we lost to the Toyama No.1, who beat us with no help at all from his partner, the PTA leader's wife. She had been drawn with Takako for the women's doubles, and they lost all their matches, so this novice was at the end awarded both the winners' and the losers' prizes! When it came to my turn to play with Mrs T, she had grown tired, so I ended up with a substitute. However, we made no headway at all. We all received small towels for taking part, and I was presented with a runners-up prize – five pairs of uselessly small tights.

The main gain for me, however, was the observations I could make of the language used. It was very casual throughout the day, with very little *keigo* to be heard at all. There were few speeches, just a brief opening and some explanation of the rules, but even here the language was pretty basic. Compared with the PTA meeting I had attended, in much the same company, there was a definite lowering of the tone. On that occasion, the participants had dressed rather smartly; here they were wearing sports gear. Since this was the first tennis tournament they had held, there was no precedent, and I felt encouraged that the style of clothing was influencing the use of language. Even Mrs T adopted a sporty level, and she was in the habit of setting the trend.

A few weeks later, a private occasion so unsettled the members of our tennis group that the language fell into no special category at all. Indeed, some of those present were reduced to giggles.

The host was Mrs Obayashi, who had telephoned the others to invite them over to a *mochiyori* – a word which could translate literally as a 'call-by, carrying', or a 'bring and share'. Takako rang me with the news, listing the others who would be present: basically our tennis group plus the new heroes, the PTA leader and his wife. She explained that we were all to take along an item of food, and if I could produce something typically English, I would be welcome to go. Takako was clearly somewhat nervous about the whole affair, unsure whether it would be worth the effort, and even dithering about whether I should phone my acceptance directly, or allow her to pass on the message.

In the end, I called Mrs Obayashi myself, and ascertained that she was planning to cook 'roast beef', so I immediately offered to make the accompanying Yorkshire pudding. Since my mother is from Yorkshire, it seemed rather appropriate. Jenny was invited too, and she suggested making a rather splendid cake we had already sampled, which featured brandy-flavoured biscuits in the middle. I made a special trip over to the house of the cookery teacher to borrow some containers for Yorkshire pudding, planning to prepare the batter and then do the cooking after our arrival at the Obayashi home. When I rang to confirm this arrangement, however, I discovered that the 'roast beef' had already been cooked and was, at that moment, ready in the fridge. Of the beef fat I would need for the Yorkshire pudding, there was none.

Clearly there had been a Japanisation of the term 'roast beef' here, and the plate of cold beef, which we were eventually served, would not have been enhanced by adding Yorkshire pudding at the last minute. I decided to make carrot soup, another of Jenny's recipes which had already gone down well at the cubs' cook-out. Meanwhile, Takako had been so concerned about what she should take that she had called round two other members of the invited group to discuss the matter over coffee. I dropped in during this gathering, but I was not really welcome, while Jenny was greatly in demand. I suspect I had possibly been classified as useless, as if I were a mere husband, but that is pure speculation.

The results of their deliberations were a combination of dishes, which Jenny was to help prepare, each of which had the following characteristics: they were originally Western, they had English names, and they proved to be quite unlike their prototype! The most appealing of them all was created by a woman who at the planning meeting had pronounced 'something simple will be fine'. She turned up with an enormous cake, constructed out of biscuits and choux pastry, in the shape of a fairy-tale (Western) cottage strongly reminiscent of that discovered by Hansel and Gretel. It was a little extra something for the children, she revealed modestly.

Takako settled on a dish of which I had never heard, namely 'Tun Stew'. It consisted of an oval plate artfully arranged with slices of cooked meat, interspersed with roast potatoes, broccoli and carrots, all spread with gravy and a sprinkling of mushrooms, but all, again, completely cold. I did give it a taste, but the 'tongue', if that is what it was, turned my stomach. It seemed designed to appeal rather to the eye than the palate, but I discovered later that it was very highly ranked that year in *Kinkonkan*, the book that Yoko had recommended about middle-class consciousness in Japan! Takako also took along a couple of bottles of Bailey's, while we made do with a bottle of white wine.

When the evening arrived, our two families, complete with children, set off at a little before six in Takako's large family vehicle, Minoru at the wheel. It is probably necessary to explain at this point that Japanese couples down to at least Takako's generation rarely went out as couples to share dinner in the Western fashion, and this was definitely an occasion planned on a Western model, as we were to see. At a point on the route, close to the central entertainment district of Toyama, Minoru drew up and jumped out, gasping something which sounded as though he could not go through with this. Takako calmly took over the driving seat, and we proceeded on our way. Not a word of explanation was offered and I wondered if he had perhaps never intended to come.

We arrived at the Obayashis' apartment, inside the hospital building, just as one of the other wives did, also accompanied only by her children. The room where we were received was enormous. At one end, the housekeeper stood by a door to the kitchen, in front of which a low table was laid out for the children, the Hansel and Gretel cake in pride of place in the middle. Off to the side was a colourfully decorated room full of toys and other attractive objects, evidently prepared to appeal to the youngsters and keep them happily occupied. A lighted Christmas tree twinkled in the centre, and, beyond, the room opened out to reveal a long keyhole-shaped table, laid with knives, forks, napkins and glasses. In each place was an oval plastic plate, divided conveniently into three sections. The centre was lit with candles (see Figure 4).

By Western standards, this was a carefully prepared dinner table, if a little unorthodox in its use of plastic crockery, but it was clearly unfamiliar to the assembled company. Dr Obayashi, the husband, invited us to sit at the table, which Jenny and I immediately did, at the distant end of the rounded section. The other adults present were more reticent, however, and Takako and the other two women laid down their plates and disappeared back to the children's area, or possibly the kitchen, for quite some time. Dr Obayashi served us drinks from a bar at the other end of the table and sat himself down in a position diametrically opposite to ours, some distance away since the table was set for fourteen. We proceeded to engage in a rather stilted conversation.

This was sparkling in comparison with the interaction which ensued when the women returned from the kitchen, however. They virtually ignored the place settings, and the three of them huddled together at the rounded end, plainly as far away as they could manage from Dr Obayashi. Toshiko, his wife, brought her beef to the table and began to serve it out. There was some hesitation about starting to eat,

Figure 4 The tennis coach, with Jenny, the anthropologist and another guest, at the 'surreal' dinner

but eventually people began picking, almost surreptitiously, at the food. The three female guests spoke only in the most formal tones across the table, but spent much of their time giggling to themselves, and whispering behind their hands. Takako's language, when it could be heard, sounded superciliously polite. The Obayashis' was quite relaxed.

Toshiko Obayashi tried her hardest to encourage people to eat and enjoy themselves, and she had clearly made every effort to create a nice atmosphere. Takako and her friends had been pleased to be asked, and they had spent some time and effort in their preparations too. They had stretched themselves to try to fit the bill, but they were reduced to embarrassment in a corner. Jenny and I were perhaps the most at ease, for the table was set out in a way which we recognised, and we were anyway in an adaptive mode, living in a foreign country. We could hardly ignore the great social gulf which seemed to gape between our hosts and their other guests, however.

As if this scene were not already bizarre enough, the men then began to arrive. First, the tennis coach, whom I thought might help to break the ice, but he was very much out of his depth. He sat the whole time in a short coat and scarf, responding nervously to the questions addressed in his direction, warming a little when they were about tennis, but seizing up when they were more general. He had spent some time in California, and he was asked about 'abroad' in awed tones. His answers were so quiet that they were inaudible at our end of the table. My male partner from the tournament turned up next, and, again, I thought we might make some jovial banter, but he was very quiet. From time to time, perhaps fortunately, the children raced through from the other end of the room and danced around the table.

At a very late stage, my carrot soup was carried in from the kitchen, suitably warmed, and, hard on its heels, the cakes and puddings, which the children were called to select from our table, as well. The soup appears last at Japanese banquets, so this was probably the rationale for waiting. At about 9.30 p.m., Takako stood up to leave, and insisted, despite much protest from the Obayashis and the wife whose husband had finally turned up. In the car, she was unquestionably relieved to be on the way home. When I asked her about Minoru, she revealed that he had chanced to drop home when she and the other two were discussing menus. He had decided he would rather play mah-jong with his friends. Had he known in advance what he would miss, he would undoubtedly have stuck by his decision.

Later, when I began to think more seriously about the 'wrapping of space', I speculated about the source of difficulty on this occasion in terms of inappropriate expectations. Takako had already lived abroad, so she should not have been fazed by the Western table setting, but she was clearly unwilling to sit down in the way she would surely have done in England. There was also a gender issue, as it was only Mr Obayashi who was seated at first, and it had for long been customary in Japanese homes for men to sit down, and for women to serve them. But the table was set for all of us. At the time, however, and probably helped by the wine, Jenny and I found the whole evening simply surreal.

Chapter 16

Concerts, cakes and spiritual communication

Consultation with religious experts brings awareness of a new aspect of language use, and reveals an unexpected association between unadorned language and unwrapped gifts.

There was a pleasant concert hall in Toyama, and we attended various events there during our stay. One was organised by White Lily, which made music a speciality, and Mrs Takahashi and her star musicians sat in the very middle of the hall, in pride of place. In the lower ranks of the audience, we were surprised by the level of informality, possibly a hangover from the days, only a generation or two before, when Japanese theatre-goers would take along a picnic, and laugh and chat during the performance. The chatter was a little off-putting to me when listening to music, but it was this degree of informality which one evening allowed me to make a very valuable contact.

I had been systematically interviewing many of my informants about their use, or otherwise, of *keigo*, and as we approached Christmas, which was over half-way through my stay, I was trying to fill in gaps in my coverage. I had started out seeking classes to visit and attend, partly because the teacher–pupil relation is often given as an example of polite language use, but I had found in my own experience that things were much more complicated than this. In my classes in Toyama, the language was not very formal, and in Tokyo I had heard professors talking about how they would be suspicious if students were too polite. I wondered whether the study of a traditional Japanese performance art, such as the koto, would influence the language used.

Mrs Ohkawa, my friend from the bank, told me that she knew a koto teacher, and she would introduce me, so we arranged to spend a

Sunday afternoon together, ending up at a concert to be given by this teacher and her pupils. Mrs Ohkawa was interested in my children, who were both playing sport that day, so we watched a little of Callum's baseball and then set off, by bus, for a neighbouring town where Hamish's soccer team had a match. She was pleased to travel there, she said, for it was her husband's home town, and a niece lived there, who came to Jenny for English classes. We watched the football, but we also, of course, had to call in on the relations. It was impossible to leave without accepting considerable hospitality, and the time for the start of the concert came and went.

Eventually, we were able to leave, and the father of the family offered to drive us back to town. On the way, we revealed our intention to go to the concert, and he was kind enough to drop us off at the door. We managed only to see the very last section, but it was quite esoteric music so I was not too concerned. Afterwards, Mrs Ohkawa kept her promise and introduced me to the koto teacher, who agreed to allow me to sit in on one of her classes. As it turned out, she was married to the shakuhachi player, Ishii Tōzan, who shared a star role in the concert, and the two of them lived in a local Buddhist temple. They were, of course, the son and daughter-in-law of the old priest I had met in his underwear.

In fact, by chance, I had an opportunity to visit their house before I managed to make an appointment for the class. The concert had been a last event before the New Year holiday, and the teacher suggested we wait until they convene again in January. Her daughter had a birthday party in the meantime, however, and she invited Hamish, who was in her class at school. I was invited to accompany him, so I met the whole family, including a sister who had moved away but returned for her niece's party. This was the artist whose work was currently on display near the station, and she took a particular interest in us because, she explained, her older sister lived in America. Over the remaining months of our stay, the whole family took an interest in us, an interest which also often contributed to the research.

The koto class was quite useful, as much for the intriguing wrapping of the instrument as for the language, which was again relatively informal. The koto, essentially a huge curved wooden structure, is carefully constructed in layers, and the strings are stretched across the convex upper surface, raised at appropriate points by a series of bridges. The ends of the instrument, at least on this occasion, were neatly wrapped in colourful brocade packets, and each player also stored her plectra in a box, kept in a similar brocade bag. I was impressed by the arrangement of space. The lack of formality in the language by no means detracted from an almost ritual air of procedure. Outdoor bags were deposited in a separate, informal part of the room (as they were at the flower-arranging class), and each player laid out her instrument, the cushion on which she sat, and the plectrum/bridge box and its bag in precisely the same relative position. There was also a formal greeting at the beginning and end of the class. It would clearly have been totally inadequate to concentrate only on the language of interaction between the teacher and her pupils to understand the formal elements of this teaching situation.

On another visit to the house, the shakuhachi player took it upon himself to introduce me to some of the deeper elements of artistic communication, both musical and visual, and he also gave me some interesting ideas about Buddhist ceremony. Ishii Tōzan was an intense man, with an impelling manner, and striking good looks. His hair was parted in the middle, unusual for a Japanese man, and he had a small triangular-shaped bruise under his bottom lip. At first, he jumped up and down, excitedly consulting books and producing illustrations of what he was saying, but as time went by, he settled down and seemed to relax. We (or rather he) talked for several hours.

He gave me a brief introduction to some of the basic tenets of Zen Buddhism, the sect he espoused, but the most interesting part, from the point of view of language, was applicable to many forms of Buddhist ceremony. The sutras which are chanted have their origins in the Sanskrit or Tibetan languages, so their meaning is incomprehensible to ordinary people in Japan, yet they will request 'long ones', as if this somehow makes them more worthwhile. This language is thus playing a role beyond its literal meaning, and it is clearly perceived to possess a certain ritual power. I suggested a parallel with the way the words of the fixed *keigo* used in ceremony has little meaning, and he agreed. The language of sutras is even more fixed and formal, and has even less meaning for the lay person.

Playing the shakuhachi is at the other end of the communication scale, however, he argued. He drew a comparison between this traditional Japanese instrument and the Western flute, a comparison which he eventually extrapolated to cover other forms of Japanese and Western art. The Western flute has many holes and other devices, and it is very functional and rational, he said, but the shakuhachi has only five holes. Similarly, oil painting involves many colours and layers of paint, whereas *sumie* ink painting has only the one medium. In each case, the Japanese version allows more scope for depth of expression, he explained.

I was somewhat surprised by this assertion, since Takako had criticised the pianist at the White Lily concert for being too emotional, whereas I had thought her work very moving. Takako had explained on that occasion that Japanese people prefer technical competence to an overkill on the expressive side. The emotion was perhaps too obvious, came the answer, though when I later went to hear Ishii Tōzan's shakuhachi playing in Tokyo, I was struck by the degree of emotion with which he imbued his work. It is a communication of deep artistry, he persisted, only truly recognisable by another with the same depth. One needs 'control', he said, using the English word, to plumb one's own depths and understand those of others. I found this idea of communication beyond language appealing, and I began to understand the advantage of limiting the medium of expression.

After the Tokyo concert, I happened to meet Ishii-*san* on the train on the way back, and he invited me round to share some special cakes he was bringing. Until I arrived, I had no inclination of just what a cake (or, perhaps, dessert) could become, and I realised that on this occasion it was they which formed the artistic medium. They were quite amazing. The edible part consisted only in a preserved plum, suspended in jelly, in a little pot, but each pot was placed on a four-legged umbrella stand, supporting a canopy of pink textured paper. At one corner, a single yellow jasmine flower was fixed with a sprig of three-spined pine, a species apparently found only on one sacred mountain in the west of Japan. The whole was finished by a small bell, hanging above the cake, under the canopy.

We ate them in style, seated rather formally, with another Buddhist priest and a friend of Mrs Ishii, the koto player. We were served ceremonial tea after eating the cake, then a cup of black tea. Later we were brought sushi for lunch, more tea, and two further kinds of cake. The substance of these was sweet red beans, wrapped in paper, and another kind of jelly, also wrapped, with a third kind of jelly inside it. Everyone seemed to think them quite delicious, though I was more impressed by the wrapping. We had to spend some time after the feast, listening to a rerun of the shakuhachi part of the concert, at a volume so loud that the speakers were buzzing, but it was a small price to pay for such an ostentatious expression of nutritional display.

I had been turning over in my mind for some time whether I could incorporate food into the wrapping scheme. The use of different kinds of Western food had clearly been important at the 'surreal' dinner, and its appearance had seemed more communicative than its taste. Trays of special food, served at weddings and other ceremonial occasions, are aesthetically pleasing as well as symbolic, and our last cooking class before the New Year holiday was devoted to delicacies appropriate for this time of year. Several times, I had found myself practising the art of enclosing one type of edible material in another, or learning how to separate different layers of food so that the result would be a pleasing combination of colour and texture.

I fell to thinking how often food for special occasions is literally one substance wrapped in another, and I remembered how in department stores models of cakes on display show how the inside will look when opened. Cakes purchased for a present will often be individually wrapped in paper, or sometimes a leaf, further packed into a box, which is itself wrapped again, and the whole placed in a carrier bag (see Figure 5). Several varieties of sushi are wrapped or rolled, and a favourite Japanese dish is tempura, a variety of vegetables and sometimes fish, dipped in batter to form a packet when it is deep-fried. Perhaps the degree of wrapping a food displays can again indicate a level of formality, or social status. This would explain the expensive individually wrapped biscuits my housewives served at their coffee mornings.

An interesting variation on this theme emerged when I went to interview the Shinto priests at the Awa Shrine, a few miles away down the peninsula. I had been invited by Hosaka-san (Rehabili) to join him at a harvest festival, when many offerings of grain, fruit and vegetables were presented to the deities, piled up on ceremonial wooden stands. It had been a solemn ceremony, presided over by a grand priest from the main shrine at Ise, and accompanied by ancient court music played on the flute and ceremonial drums. It was clearly an important civic occasion, too, for the mayor was present, as well as a number of other Toyama dignitaries. It was a wonderful opportunity to observe the use of ceremonial language, and I asked the local priests if I could follow up the event with a visit to inquire further into the language of Shinto ritual.

They had agreed readily enough, and I spent a morning of fascinating exploration into the parallels and comparisons with forms of language I had already observed. The language of prayer, or *norito*, shares some of the characteristics of the Buddhist sutras in that it has a ritual and, indeed, spiritual power, but its literal meaning is beyond the comprehension of the ordinary participant. This time it is ancient Japanese language, which predates the arrival of religious dogma from

Figure 5 Cakes may not only come in several layers of wrapping, but also consist of substances wrapped around each other

mainland Asia, unchanged for the 1,200 years since Chinese script was imported to record it, they explained. Its use thus plays a ceremonial role, appreciated by the lay worshipper for its form rather than its content, but there the similarity wanes it seems.

From the point of view of the Shinto priests, this is the language of prayer, words of address to the gods. I asked about its level of respect. Was it perhaps similar to the language used to address the emperor? One of the priests present pointed out immediately that ordinary people don't usually have the opportunity to address the emperor, whereas they do expect to speak to the gods. The high level of respect language due to members of the imperial family serves to isolate and protect them (as do the dense surroundings of the palaces in which they live, I mused), but Shinto shrines encourage the possibility of communication. The priests mediate that communication during ritual, but people can call upon the gods at any time.

Next, I asked about levels of politeness, and they explained that communication with the gods is different from the social interaction of daily life. It comes from the inside of the body, from the spirit or soul, and is conveyed directly, without any need for embellishment. In some ways, this makes the gods much closer than other human beings, one pointed out. I suddenly realised that communication from the *inside of the body* would be totally unwrapped, so if *keigo* can be thought of as a wrapping around real feelings, this spiritual communication would be the exact opposite. My first ideas had been unconsciously and ethno-centrically drawing parallels with the language I had been brought up to use in communicating with the God of my own Christian faith.

Almost instantly, I remembered the way that offerings made to the gods are usually presented unwrapped. At the harvest festival, I had observed pile upon pile of different varieties of food, open on their little ceremonial tables. At a house-building ceremony, a short walk from our house, I had photographed the offerings of rice, fresh fruit and even fish, open to the warm sunshine in which they stood (see Figure 6). The sake bottles were wrapped, but this could hardly be poured out over the altar. I asked the priests about offerings, and they confirmed that these should properly be made unwrapped. They are different from gifts, they explained; they are presented to the gods as food, and if people bring them in paper, they should remove it when they arrive. Even the sake should be poured into special pots.

This revelation was another major high point in my research. It

Figure 6 Offerings to the gods, here at the site of a new building, should properly be made unwrapped

drew the use of food firmly into the wrapping scheme, and opened up a spiritual aspect of communication which would occupy my thoughts every time I entered a shrine or temple during our stay, and in the months of analysis which followed. The Awa priests answered questions on several other subjects on this and a subsequent visit, and much of their information was independently confirmed by the female Shinto priest at the shrine near our old Toyama home when I went to call on her. From that moment, the wrapping phenomenon, as I came to call it, took firm root, and I moved with some confidence into a mode of developing and filling out the ideas.

Part IV

Building a framework
for analysis

Chapter 17

New Year

Shrine, *mochi* and a tea ceremony

> Joining in with local festivities at New Year provides encouragement
> for developing ideas and brings a new mood of confidence to the
> project.

It was entirely appropriate, by Japanese standards, to move into a new
phase of research at the New Year, for this is the biggest holiday in
Japan, and it is taken very seriously. People make every effort to clear
all outstanding business, pay their debts, tidy their homes, workshops
and offices, and set up decorations for the festive season. Housewives
prepare food for several days so that they, too, can take a break from
their usual work, and New Year activities run on well into January.
Groups of workmates and friends celebrate the end of the old year,
largely by drinking together, and they celebrate the beginning of the
New Year in the same way. Various special interest groups have their
own events too.

A period such as this is no holiday for an anthropologist, of course,
for the festive activity is full of symbolism and special language, and
the customs which are practised can only be observed once each year.
It was not my first New Year in Japan, and I was able to anticipate the
flurry of invitations we would receive, and the note-taking I would
make, so we booked a family skiing holiday over the quieter Christmas.
That in itself was an education. We chose a package holiday in
Hokkaido, which is said to be less crowded than the Japan Alps, and
the flights, bus journeys and hotels all offered opportunities to listen to
the polite language of our guides and other caretakers. The language of
the ski slopes was interesting, too, but it was the deference that a relatively small sum of money will buy that particularly impressed me. The
customer is treated well in Japan.

Back in Toyama, we were surprised by how early everything closed down on New Year's Eve. We had planned to eat out, but the first restaurant we approached had closed at 6 p.m., and as we walked along the side streets we watched people come out from house after house to put up their *kadomatsu*, a decoration for the front door, and affix smaller versions on the front of their newly cleaned cars. Cafés and restaurants decorated their entrances with standing arrangements of bamboo and pine, finished at the base with a new, twisted rope, apparently symbolic of the plum which completes a trio of plants to bring good fortune. These were handsome affairs, which I admired until I learned that they were often sold at exorbitant rates by members of the *yakuza*.

We found the local version of McDonald's open, at last, but otherwise only barbers, hairdressers and fishmongers were working late on that particular evening, supplying everyone with the wherewithal to present themselves appropriately on the first morning of the year. I remembered that some years previously, in the country, I had brought in the New Year, at midnight, with a neighbour in the bathhouse. Some of us had been down to the local temple to ring out the 108 bells of old sins, but everyone dispersed to their homes before the bewitching hour, which was clearly not particularly significant. In Japan, the New Year starts with a fresh morning; it is not customary to blot oneself into a stupor the night before, as is commonly the case in Scotland, my family home.

In Toyama, we followed the local custom on 1 January of making a visit to Awa Shrine, with which I was now quite familiar. This was a time-consuming process, for the road was completely full of vehicles whose passengers had the same intention. Our bus drew to a halt some three kilometres before the shrine, according to the driver, although I think he exaggerated a little. The atmosphere was good, however, and people were greeting one another gaily, so it did not seem as tedious as such a predicament might have done on an ordinary day. Eventually, as the bus edged slowly forward, we decided to walk the last few hundred yards, and arrived well before our fellow-passengers.

The procedure, once inside the shrine, seemed to be to go up to the inner shrine to pray, to throw an offering into the box, and then to return to the rows of special stalls to buy some protection for the coming year. There was a colourful variety of amulets and talismans, but the most popular objects on sale were evidently decorated arrows, which would symbolically direct their owners with purpose into the coming year. Behind the stalls, a row of *miko* (shrine maidens), dressed in bright red and white robes, were lined up to attend to the endless stream of customers. There was also a huge fire burning, so that last year's paraphernalia could be cast away, for the power of these sacred objects lasts only one year.

Another popular custom is to write a wish for the year on a little wooden plaque, known as an *ema*, and hang it up for the attention of the deities, along with hordes of others like it. Just outside the shrine were rows of chubby, round-faced dolls called *daruma*, their vacant eyes waiting to be painted in, one at the time of a wish being expressed, the other on its accomplishment. A selection of stalls offered food and drink to the cheerful visitors, and some had set up a range of toys to attract the attention of passing children. New Year is a time when small envelopes containing quite substantial sums of money are handed over to the youngsters of the family, and these stall-keepers never miss a chance. Visits to shrines in Japan continue through the first three days of the year, and judging by the queue of cars which came right back to the hospital on the second, that was an even more popular day than the first.

New Year is also a time for renewing old acquaintance, and we were invited to visit some friends who live near our former home, where a special celebration takes place on the second. This is an interesting custom, called *mikan-nage*, literally throwing oranges, which is precisely what it involves. Owners of all the boats in the harbour carry boxes of oranges up into the tall, proud bows, and after a prayer and an offering of sake, they, or more often their children, hurl the fruit to the waiting crowds below. The principle is to give abundantly away, to ensure good catches for the coming year, it was explained, and oranges are chosen because these are grown in Wakayama prefecture, whose shores are visible from one of the favourite fishing grounds.

The same 'throwing principle' underlies other customary practices in Japan, like throwing rice cakes off the roof of a newly built house, so that the neighbours can come round and share in the celebration; and casting beans out of the house on *Setsubun*, the first day of spring, to symbolise the casting out of devils, and the encouragement of good fortune into the home. It is an important part of the culture of reciprocity, which also explains much of the abundant gift-giving. At New Year and Midsummer, many gifts change hands, and huge sums of money are spent in what is seen as an investment, at least in social relations. The purchase of protective objects at the shrine is also an investment, to ensure safety in the home and elsewhere.

After the ceremony, we were invited to the home of our friends' relatives, in the heart of the fishing community. The alcove in the main room was decorated with a variety of preserved fish, some tightly bound in straw, others wrapped with rope, each symbolic of some aspect of the good fortune sought for the New Year. We had met this family once before, during the summer of our earlier stay, when they had taken us out into the bay in their boat to get a good view of a firework display. The view had been excellent, but the weather less than perfect, and I had felt very sick, so it was not a memory I cherished. The family was welcoming again, however, and they began to prepare all kinds of delicious food.

Various relatives called round during the course of the day, and there was much drinking and jollification. I was able to meet several people whom I had known only briefly before, and I set up some interviews for the coming weeks. These people were true locals of the district, and they were able to illustrate and answer questions about the use of language in a way which I had only learned second-hand before. For example, they could tell me about the differences between the speech of several fishing communities, and how this differed again from the language of the farming villages further inland. They could also explain the way they alter their language when speaking to outsiders, and slip into a stronger form of local dialect when with friends. They had little time for *keigo*, except on ceremonial occasions, but, curiously perhaps in view of the comments of the Awa priests, they did use a little when at prayer.

We also spent pleasant times with our old friends, the Nodas, over the holiday period. On our previous visit, we had ascertained that their chef was an interesting man who had been divorced not long since, so I decided to practise a little match-making and invite a single friend of mine from Tokyo to meet him. This is a common custom in Japan, which I had studied in some detail on my first field trip, although I cannot say that I acquired much skill. My Tokyo friend, Kazuko, is one of the people I know best in Japan, and she was willing enough to come along. She is quite a high-powered lecturer, but she had often bemoaned her single state, so it seemed a nice opportunity. The occasion took place a week or two before Christmas, and Kazuko arrived loaded with gifts.

She brought Christmas presents for all of us, and a sealed packet of cooked ham, packed in a special box, for *oseibo*, the New Year round of exchange. This latter was presented very attractively, on a satin cushion, and, as I later discovered, the price would certainly have far exceeded the value of the meat inside. This special wrapping indicates the nature of the event, and demonstrates the expenditure of a substantial sum. Indeed, it is the sum which is more important than the contents of the gift on these occasions, and the sealed nature of the meat meant that it could be preserved for some time. My relationship with Kazuko had always been rather informal up to this point, but I supposed that a match-making introduction was worth some extra investment.

Jenny prepared some good food, and we spent a pleasant evening with the Nodas and their chef. Kazuko seemed in good form, as did the chef, and they exchanged name cards before parting. The imminent opening of the *pension* would allow Kazuko an opportunity to make a future visit, I thought, although I don't know if she ever made it. A couple of years later, when Kazuko celebrated her fortieth birthday, she told me rather solemnly that she was now resigned to being single, and she would devote herself to her career. That objective she has certainly pursued with vigour. For ourselves, we received an invitation from the Nodas to visit at New Year, and witness the practice known as *mochitsuki*, a traditional method of pounding rice to make the ubiquitous New Year *mochi* cakes.

This was an excellent outing, for not only did we have a chance to take a turn at the pounding, but I also ascertained another important aspect of the wrapping phenomenon. As might be expected, the Nodas did everything in style, and, when we arrived, the rice was being steamed over a wooden fire in the compound, its authentic wooden containers suspended over gently bubbling water. We were picked up by the artist who was helping design aspects of the Nodas' *pension*, and we had both chosen strawberries to take as a gift. The main difference, however, was that hers were unwrapped beyond the functional punnets, whereas mine were, as I thought, properly contained in wrapping paper. She explained that, as an insider to the house, wrapping was unnecessary. It was an expression of intimacy to leave them unwrapped. This was an important point to learn, nicely complementing communication with the spirit world.

The *mochitsuki* itself involved a serious rhythmic procedure, with two participants alternately wielding large wooden mallets over a stone container. The movements are interspersed with quick adjustments to the glutinous mass below (see Figure 7), which looked quite foolhardy, but seemed to illustrate genuine Japanese cooperation and trust. The resulting soft mass was fashioned into rice cakes, or *mochi*, which we ate with an odorous dish of fermented beans, known as *natto*, and a liquid extracted from the *daikon*, a large white radish commonly used in Japanese cuisine. The feast was accompanied by home-distilled sake, made with fresh water from a well, further up the hill. It was an experience to titillate the taste buds, but I have to say that we were quite pleased to reach the more familiar taste of the strawberries which followed.

Another culinary experience which arose at New Year was quite a surprise. My flower-arranging teacher rang me up and invited me to an event called *hatsugama*, a first tea ceremony, which I accepted willingly enough, and, as it turned out, rather innocently. Many events following the New Year are called *hatsu* one thing or another, for this simply means 'first', and the literal translation of 'gama' is 'kettle', so I had no inkling of the exquisite feast we would be served, except that she invited me to arrive at noon. At this stage, I had not even read much about the tea ceremony, so I was unprepared for the formality and, indeed, the length of the ritual which followed.

I arrived a little early, as it turned out, and I was shown into the usual tea room, which was referred to as the 'waiting area' on this occasion, where I did indeed wait for the other guests. There were to be three, and once they had arrived we went back out of the front door and into the garden, where we washed our hands and rinsed our mouths from a little stone pool using a wooden pourer. We then proceeded through the garden, along stepping stones in the grass, and entered a sliding door at the back, which had been left slightly ajar to indicate the way. From the wooden verandah, we entered the main room, one by one, on our knees, bowing to no one in particular, and then moving round to admire the scroll and flowers in the alcove, and take our places beside the tea utensils.

We had decided on the order of entry in the waiting room, but it was the most senior pupil who led the way, followed by the second, so I had two examples before me, which was just as well in view of the formality involved. Once we were seated, the teacher appeared, greeted us with a deep bow, and proceeded to serve trays of special food for the occasion. Our leader invited her to join us, but she refused, returning only to serve ceremonial sake. The food was delicious, though it was not always possible for me to identify what exactly it was, beyond a general tendency to rice and fish products. We were expected to eat it all up, according to our leader, and then wipe out the box and bowls with the paper always carried on these occasions. As we laid down our chopsticks, the host would know we were ready, she explained.

Indeed, the trays were then removed, and we were served cakes for the first tea ceremony. These were passed around, but before we took

Figure 7 The anthropologist tries her hand at
pounding rice, while the host bravely
adjusts the mixture between blows
and Callum looks on

tea, there was a period of relaxation and photography in the garden.
There were two ceremonies, one with a common cup, the other with a
separate cup served to each of us, and the teacher jogged our leader to
comment on the flowers, scroll, pottery, and so forth. At the end, we
retreated through the garden, back to the waiting room, where we had
left our bags, and the other pupils prepared to pay for the occasion.
The teacher reappeared, in a more relaxed mode, and brought a box for
us to share between us. It contained punnets of strawberries, which she
suggested we take home, but the others refused, and eventually we ate
them informally in the waiting room.

The atmosphere during this last part of the day was in marked contrast to the rest. At last, people spoke in normal voices, rather than the hushed tones which had characterised the ceremonial, and after a few laughs and giggles, we prepared to leave. It was not far off four o'clock. Two days later, I went along for my first tea lesson, though I can't for the life of me remember whether I committed myself to this before or after the occasion of *hatsugama*.

Chapter 18

Valentine's Day, and the 6th years pick on Hamish

Travel to an old fieldwork site opens up a regional dimension to the research, a school meeting suggests an idea about the wrapping of time, and further family problems add useful information to the findings.

As normal life resumed, my interviews continued, and I gathered a good range of views on the use of language, and now wrapping. Toyama had proved to be an excellent choice for my research, for the different groups of people who lived in and around the town illustrated a wide variety of ways in which *keigo* was, or was not, used, and the contact between these groups made people aware of their own idiosyncrasies. Particularly useful was an interview with a White Lily mother whose family ran a motor repair business, because she was both aware of the advantages of adjusting her levels of politeness to make people feel comfortable, and articulate about how she did this. The expensive furnishings in her home may have been testimony to her success in attracting and keeping her family's custom.

In February, I made a trip to Kyushu, where I had previously worked for a year, to carry out some comparative work in a different part of the country, and this exercise served to emphasise even further the value of the cosmopolitan location. Kyushu is home to some quite strong dialects, but they are regarded more positively than in Toyama, and the local council where I had worked was so concerned their particular version should not die out that they were giving free dialect card games to all the local children. *Keigo* has its dialect version, too, but it is used little in everyday life, for in more closed communities people only rarely meet strangers. They do use it for ceremonial occasions, however.

When I began to think seriously about the variations in language and politeness based on dialect, region and social class, I became more and more convinced that similar principles of analysis could be applied. In every case, the differences in language serve to identify social groups, which 'wrap themselves' in usage comfortable within the group, but adjust them outside. In an area where there is little contact with the outside, it is levels of formality and ceremonial which are marked, and I had already seen these used as a model for class difference. In a cosmopolitan area such as Toyama, the dialect, which is often described as 'rough', or 'dirty', has become opposed to the more refined language of Tokyo. In practice, of course, Tokyo has rough language too, but there it is distinguished as 'lower-town', and opposed to the language of the 'upper mountain'. In both cases, regional difference is being used to rationalise a basic class distinction.

It was clearly a good idea to study the continuum of language, as well as that of wrapping, and I discovered that there is an opposite of politeness known as 'naked speech', which links in well with the wrapping metaphor. It is not necessarily abusive, as rough English might be, but it is rather curt and direct. In fact, I had two excellent informants under my own roof, for small boys spend little time adorning their speech with niceties, and Hamish was after all very close to members of the underworld. I encouraged him to invite his friends to visit, but my presence tended to constrain their communication, so I decided to give him a tape recorder to gather some of their more informal chat. The boys were delighted, and I acquired a whole new set of vocabulary, which I personally, as an adult woman, could hardly use.

An incident one day, when I was cycling along a side street with Callum on the back seat of my bike, gave me a chance to hear it, however. A high school boy whom we passed called out 'Herro', a common greeting to foreigners, simply a mispronunciation of 'Hello'. Callum, tired of hearing the word, replied 'Baka', meaning something close to 'Stupid'. The boy was quick, because we hardly slowed down, and came back with another word of the same order, 'Aho' ('Fool'), to which Callum responded, equally fast, 'Manuke' ('Blockhead'). 'Oh, it's Hamish,' called the boy, for Hamish had something of a reputation for his colloquial language. 'No, it's Callum,' came the reply. 'Callum is baka,' the boy persisted. 'No, I'm not, bye bye,' yelled Callum, cheerfully, as we swung around the corner. No malice, no politeness, and they were both laughing.

The school connection was useful in other ways too. A PTA meeting, for example, made me aware of a kind of temporal version of the wrapping principle where different speech levels were appropriate for different parts of the meeting. It opened with several formal greetings, which involved much *keigo*, but words with little content, like thanks for turning out when you must be so busy, and general appeals for parental cooperation. The second part announced the subjects of the day's meeting, though the language was still rather stilted, and the speaker's invitation to comments from the audience was clearly not to be taken up at that moment. The third part, by contrast, was devoted to discussion, and here the local dialect came out in full force.

At tea with a couple of friends afterwards, I commented that the officials of the PTA would need to be conversant with *keigo* to introduce the meeting, and they added that the officials usually choose their successors so it is something of a closed shop. The roles are usually played by the parents of the oldest children in the 6th year, and those with a lot of experience, so it might be hard for someone with only one child to make the grade. One of them also commented wryly that she would be unlikely to be chosen because she has a reputation for speaking her mind, not an endearing feature in a 'wrapped society', I supposed. She had already been quite outspoken in her criticism of Mrs T, and I had actually noticed her being slighted at the White Lily Bazaar.

It is quite a skilful business to strike exactly the right level of directness to achieve one's aims. Many parents sit tight in a school context, without open complaint, but groan to one another outside. Others make efforts to become involved, but don't necessarily have much impact. Some measure carefully how much they actually care about the school, or kindergarten, opprobrium, and this particular informant was such a person. She was an independent woman who ran successful children's classes in Western art, and she came from an academic family. At a strategic point, when her daughter was anyway almost through the kindergarten, she let some of her feelings, which were actually shared by many others, be publicly known.

Later, she and a group of friends invited me round to talk about education in England. These women were dissatisfied with their own system, which is of course often cited as a model in Britain, and they were interested to intervene in a way which would be effective for their own children. In return for my talk to them, they were very forthcoming about their own views, and they explained the subtle way in which these must be communicated in Japan, with a judicious use of polite dissent. They helped me to interpret the words of the teachers about my own children, to understand the criticism implicit in their apparent praise. The encouragement of individuality is much talked of in Japan, but conformity is vital to much of the scholarly success for which Japan is known. Talk of the behaviour of my children was used ostensibly to illustrate the advantages of individual differences, but covertly to highlight the disadvantages of too much deviation from the norm.

The school also drew selectively on the attendance of these two foreign boys for its own purposes. At an early stage, they invited me to help Hamish make a presentation to his whole school year. There were some 200 children lined up, and Hamish and I sat at the front, beside a globe and a couple of maps of Europe. Hamish had brought along some photographs of his school in Oxford, and these were pinned up on a board. Each of the five forms had chosen a couple of questions, and these were put to us by a representative. Hamish worked out his answer in English and I translated. At the end, Hamish was encouraged to ask questions, too, and a formal letter of thanks was read out by a girl representing the whole year. The whole event was friendly and fun. It started with a song, and ended with a game.

Later, at Christmas, Hamish was distraught because he was being excluded from the dressing of a tree the class had made. He rang me up and I went along, curious to see how Christmas was being celebrated at the school. In fact the tree was a gift being made by the class to present to another class, and the children already had clear ideas about how it was to be done. There was a formal Christmas party, with carols, skits and the exchange of presents, and the children I asked were convinced that they were involved in a very Japanese activity. One small girl drew out her diary, however, and read me the notes for Christmas Day. It recounted how, in olden times, in England, people would sit around a big fire and eat nuts and preserved fruit.

I felt slightly aggrieved, coming from the newly multi-cultural Britain, where the religious background of the children in a class is at least respected, and sometimes used to encourage a knowledge and toleration of different beliefs and customs. The teacher told me that Christmas in Japan is just fun, and she saw no need to explain the religious significance it might have elsewhere, if indeed she knew it. Hamish could have been asked to explain his own understanding of the feast, but on this occasion he wasn't. Two children I asked told me solemnly that 'Silent Night' and 'Jingle Bells' were ancient Japanese songs. I suppose by their standards, at age 9, they almost were. They have been sung in Japan for a good many years now.

Valentine's Day was another occasion for putting the foreigners in their place. For some weeks before, the shops displayed attractive boxes of chocolates of various sizes, though usually with the volume of wrapping material far outweighing that of the chocolate. My two decided to present gifts to their favourite girl friends, but their intentions were roundly mocked by our neighbours. Valentine's Day is for girls to give gifts to boys, we were told, and their gifts were returned. They did receive several, though, which cheered them, but they chose to ignore the custom, said to have been invented by a Japanese chocolate maker, to reciprocate the gifts they received on 14 March, known locally as 'White Day'. It is sometimes difficult to chase up cultural adaptation, but Christmas and Valentine's Day both seem to have quite clear roots in their commercial value.

Teachers at the boys' school were of course under considerable stress in having to cope with these foreigners. It was a first experience for both of them, and all their other charges had been well trained by Japanese parents and kindergartens to comply with their expectations. From time to time they invited parents in for personal interviews about their children, and on one occasion, several months after our arrival, Callum's teacher admitted to finding it difficult to adhere to the headmaster's directive to be nice to Callum so that he would take a good impression back to England. She appealed to me to apply some of the pressure a Japanese mother would to encourage him to comply.

Callum was probably an angel, however, compared to Hamish, whose teacher sent regular missives about his behaviour. She was immensely patient, despite her apparent youth, and I enjoyed our meetings, which were sometimes also quite useful for the research. At the personal interview, she made an interesting and rather sympathetic comment about Hamish's relationship with the son of the gang-leader. Hamish's acquisition of colloquial vocabulary had been more fruitful than his grasp of diplomacy, and she told me that she had caught him teasing Akira about his father's activities. She urged me to put a stop to this. 'The boy is not responsible for his parents,' she added, earnestly, and I truly believe she applied the same even-handed treatment to Hamish.

Hamish ran into trouble with his friends sometimes, although he was mostly rather popular, not least amongst the girls. One day he arrived home flushed and angry, though there was no clear explanation, and a few minutes later a couple of girls called round to warn me that the 6th year boys had been ganging up on him. Hamish was in the 4th year, but girls from the 6th year often came to see us (perhaps initially through curiosity since the 6th year is when they learn of the world outside Japan), and I wondered if the boys were jealous. It seemed that a group of them had surrounded Hamish and threatened him, one had kicked him, and they had also gone off with the key to his bicycle. These were boys from the football team, with whom he was normally on good terms, so I decided to go out and see if I could ascertain the problem.

I found the group quite quickly, but they were not immediately keen to talk to me either. Eventually, the one who had kicked Hamish came over and began to recite a catalogue of small misdemeanours. None added up to much alone, but together they represented a lack of respect due from younger boys to older ones. Most serious, it seemed, was the way Hamish boarded the football bus. The custom here was that the younger boys boarded first, but they filled up from the front, leaving the back for the older ones. The real tough guys of the 6th year, of course, took pride of place on the very back seat. Hamish had violated this unwritten rule, and they were unprepared to accept this. Hamish needed to learn, he told me.

I reasoned that Hamish had come from a society where the rules are different, and it took time to learn. It was unkind of them to gang up on him, I said. His response was quick, and interesting. 'He's living here now,' quipped the boy. We all rode away, with nothing apparently resolved, but I was able to explain their worries to Hamish, and he reassured me that the boys in his own year were on his side. Perhaps he had been encouraging wider dissent. Who knows? It is all very well for one strange boy to act oddly, but if the rot spreads further, the whole system could be threatened, and it was a role of the sixth years, and apparently their parents, to maintain the appropriate standards.

At an earlier stage I might have been upset by this incident, but the boys had only treated Hamish as they would a Japanese boy who stepped out of line, and in a way it was flattering. Like me, he had moved into a role which was not easily classified. A proper foreigner can be treated like a child, or an idiot, but a person who speaks Japanese should also respect Japanese rules of hierarchy. Hamish was in a liminal position, with some knowledge, but who knew how much? Such a situation spells danger in any society, and the boys were perhaps expressing a youthful version of Professor Suzuki's psychological torture.

Chapter 19

The gang-leader's wife

As findings fall into place, an early dilemma begins to make new sense, and adds obliquely to the research.

Japan is often described as a homogeneous society, and the bullying we witnessed in the last chapter is cited as a way in which children, and adults, learn to conform. My study of language had helped me to see that outward conformity can mask a huge variety of personal differences, that distinctions in the use of language mark off a good range of social groups, and that judicious use of speech levels can confer considerable status and power. My initial inspiration had been to investigate this last quality in the behaviour of Mrs Takahashi, but during the course of the research I had encountered plenty of other examples, and I had broadened my interest to include other types of wrapping.

The family of the Zen Buddhist temple not only illustrated these skills themselves, each member individually, but through the artist sister I finally had an opportunity to observe at closer quarters more of the wrapping distinctions of the gang-leader's circle. For the Ishii family itself, it was not only the physical wrapping. The older priest had an impressive demeanour, even in his underwear, and the younger one had a very striking posture, crowned by his unusual hairstyle. Mrs Ishii did not stand out in a crowd, but the way she served those amazing cakes betrayed a good measure of careful training in feminine arts of care for visitors, and she was clearly respected in musical circles.

Her low-key, subtle control is characteristic of Japanese women, housewives in particular, and the Western visitor is apt to mistake skills at service for the subservience they often feel Japanese women suffer. This household had only one woman to take care of two quite demanding men, but she also pursued a successful musical career. I gained little inside knowledge about the personal relations of this particular family, but of those I knew better, the outside commitment to appropriate presentation, which includes service, reveals background and upbringing, but little in the way of ideology or relative power. Indeed, those who are skilled at presentation are also usually skilled at handling personal relations as well.

Experience with Takako's housewives' *nakama* was very valuable from this point of view, for during their informal meetings these women openly discussed the management of their husbands, parents-in-law and other relations, and backed one another up with advice and support. Those who seemed most deferential on public occasions, such as the School Sports Day and the White Lily Bazaar, often proved to be amongst the most powerful in their control of family life. The maintenance of a quiet and apparently innocuous appearance, or wrapping, was indeed probably vital to the pursuit of their aims, as I was beginning to learn. There are, however, exceptions.

The sisters of the Zen priest both stand out from the norm, but neither needs to deal with married life. We only met one, at their niece's birthday party; the other had moved off to make her life in the US, and later Canada, as a scientist. She was divorced from her Japanese husband. Masumi, the artist, was single, and she chatted of her artistic lifestyle. Unlike most Japanese, who rise early to travel to work, and play in the evenings, she had formed the habit of sitting up painting through the night and sleeping in the daytime. She had studied with a famous artist in Tokyo, and was gaining a good reputation. She was currently exhibiting her work in a gallery near the station.

During the latter part of January we had visited her exhibition, which comprised many fine works, mostly on the three themes of horses, flowers and waterfalls. We had admired them, and taken tea with her in the gallery. When she learned that we had all had some riding experience, she invited us to join her one day at the stables she used in Toyama, and this gave me an opportunity to observe a different kind of Japanese social behaviour. It took some time to set up the arrangements, but towards the end of March the day came, and she picked us up in her car.

Our arrival was at first disappointing, for the place was unprepossessing, and we were to take turns to ride one horse around a muddy circle, enclosed by a fence. All the animals seemed nervous and edgy, and our chosen steed was no exception. While he was being groomed, however, we were diverted by the arrival of a couple of extraordinary-looking women. One was wearing bright green leather trousers, tightly finished at the ankle, and the other sported a riding hat which was tilted almost to touch her neatly protruding nose. The first came swaggering over, calling 'Hi' gaily to Hamish, and asking Jenny, in unfaltering American English, whether she liked riding. She caught sight of me, and after a quick second glance at Hamish, she realised who we were. This was the mother of Akira, Hamish's *yakuza* friend. We had met previously, but only briefly, at a school visit day.

It appeared that the stables were used to care for privately owned horses, rather than offering a range to be hired, hence the availability of only that of our host. The gang-leader's wife had dropped in to visit her husband's mount, an enormous beast with a fearsome expression and its mane trimmed to an aggressive-looking crew cut. It had just been ridden, but not by her husband. She spoke to the animal, engaged in some bantering with the owner, and then came back over to chat to Hamish, asking him various questions, and throwing back to the others information about his friendship with her son. She confided to me that she was thinking of sending Akira to study in England, and I trotted out the usual invitation, wondering at the same time how serious she was.

We continued to chat for some time, in fact, exchanging views on a range of issues. I was particularly struck by her confidence. Unlike most of the Japanese mothers I met, who giggled nervously in the presence of a foreigner and frequently became tongue-tied, despite discovering I could speak Japanese, she ploughed straight in, switching deftly from one language to the other. Her English was not very accurate, but she had no qualms about using it, and I am sure that she impressed those standing around as completely fluent. Her whole demeanour was brash and bold, and I suddenly became aware of the tremendous new power released by someone who has enough gall to ignore the deferential behaviour which characterises the general population.

I had heard that both she and her husband have university degrees, but then so did several of my housewifely acquaintances, some at a postgraduate level. They probably also had experience abroad, but, again, so did Takako and Yoko, and they certainly avoided any behaviour which might be regarded as brash or bold. No, this was quite a different kind of confidence, and in a society where it is the norm to display a public image of deference and conformity, on which one's skill in social life depends, this clearly brought our new acquaintance into another ball-game entirely.

This did not mean that the gang-leader's wife lacked the ability to adapt to situations, however, for at our previous meeting she had been in a tracksuit not unlike those of other mothers, she wore no make-up, and she had her hair plaited neatly down her back. In comparison with the image presented at the riding school, where her hair flew free and her face was positively masked in make-up, she had seemed to be making an effort to be inconspicuous. This is an interesting quality of Japanese *yakuza*, which is often depicted in films. Many of them demonstrate their commitment to the cause, as they see it, by having tattoos engraved over almost their whole bodies. The trick, however, is to keep completely clear those parts of the arms, legs and neck, which are visible in public, so that they can pass unnoticed when wearing normal clothes, just as their front-line occupation masks their underworld activities.

In films, a crucial moment may involve the sudden revealment of a portion of the tattoo, perhaps by dropping the shoulder of a kimono, anyway an aggressive gesture. I learned later, when I took up a short investigation of Japanese tattoos, that the whole idea of adorning the skin in this way is perceived very negatively by mainstream Japanese, who think of it as disgusting, unjustifiable damage to the body. The act of tattooing is thus a kind of rebellious bodily wrapping parallel to the brash use of dress and language I witnessed in the gang-leader's wife. In both cases, a member of the society which observes the wider norm would be shocked, and frightened, by such blatant disregard for convention.

A foreigner falls into the same category in some ways, of course, as I had observed when I met the psychiatric patient, and I was aware of the possibility of manipulating a situation of uncertainty in those I met in Japan. It is not my style to pursue this apparent advantage, however, for I feel that I learn more by trying to build up relations of goodwill, but it is possible that Hamish had been using this approach, perhaps without knowing it. His friendship with Akira would have helped, perhaps, and is also probably explained by the fact that they were both outsiders to the mainstream society from which many of their classmates came.

At around this time I visited an old friend from our previous stay in Toyama, recovering in hospital from a minor operation, and we chatted about the riding incident. She recognised the power bestowed by a disregard for convention, and described the subtlety of the protection 'offered' by the *yakuza*. Apparently, burly members of the gang would visit bars, small restaurants and sushi shops, offering items such as framed pictures for the walls, potted plants for the entrance, and the lovely New Year decorations at prices way beyond their market value. If refused, groups of these same characters would simply lurk about outside, or take up seats and order very little, their dress and hairstyle giving away their allegiance, and their threatening attitude deterring the ordinary customer. They were not breaking any existing laws (though these have since been tightened up), and most people would feel obliged to buy their wares.

My friend was also well informed about the gang rivalry in the town, and she recounted the incident which had brought the currently dominant group into its position of power. It had evidently been a simple shooting, which took place in the main hospital. The *oyabun* had been admitted for a minor injury, but while he was there, a member of the rival gang had simply walked in and murdered him. This had been the last straw for the older group, and without its head, it fell into decline. The only son of the dead man had been in primary school at the time, and he had continued to live in the town with his mother, but now he had left to go to university. He was very bright, she said, and she felt sure he would return to avenge his father's death. Perhaps even the man who had lost his hand, in an attempt to blow up the present *oyabun*'s boat, was working for him.

This story explained a tale I had heard on the hospital grapevine about the present *oyabun*, Akira's father, who had caused a stir when he was admitted to hospital by insisting on moving an existing patient out of a private room so that he could be guarded by his underlings. Now I realised why. Before we left, I heard that he had been arrested. It was not clear what he had done blatantly to disobey the laws he had been so careful to observe ostensibly, as leader, but the local police box confirmed that he was at least temporarily in gaol.

A few years after this trip, I met my friend again, when Hamish renewed his acquaintance with the youngest of her four sons, with whom he had been at kindergarten, and she told me, sadly, that her third son had joined the *yakuza*. Perhaps a little too much knowledge had proved a dangerous thing, but then this move could also have brought protection to Hamish's friend, who had set up a sushi shop. I didn't push it further, for we were meeting at White Lily Kindergarten, where all four boys had attended music and English classes, and she may not have been totally open. That will be a subject to investigate later. I never did pursue my relationship with the gang-leader's wife, and to date, Akira has not been to visit us in Britain, though Hamish has not forgotten him.

In my own progress of collecting information for the research, by the time of the riding expedition I had moved well into the phase, which I recognised from previous trips, of being able to slip new information into slots already created by the ideas I had been putting together. It is a positive and encouraging phase, for the framework which has been gradually taking shape is now filling out into a coherent whole. To use a jigsaw metaphor, the edge pieces were complete, and I had identified the main features of the picture, so new pieces were becoming easier to place. There were still some large areas of sky, and possibly sea, to work out, but they had a role in the overall scheme. The *yakuza* could be left in peace, or war!

Chapter 20

Unwrapping the argument

Another boost of confidence results from presenting ideas to the local anthropological community – and the physical nature of the commitment is revealed.

A big test came for the scheme of analysis I was putting together when I was invited to talk to the anthropology research group at Keio, the university to which I was attached. My initial sponsor, who had introduced me to Professor Suzuki and his linguistic research centre, was my old anthropology supervisor, Professor Yoshida, who is well known in the field. He had retired from Tokyo University, but held two new, part-time posts at Keio and Seishin Joshi, and it was he who gave me the opportunity to observe the different forms of language used in each. He had an interesting group of students, and he suggested that I present my ideas about wrapping to them. The seminar would also be attended by other interested academics.

It did seem a good idea, for it would be a chance to try out the scheme with an informed audience of Japanese native speakers before I invested too much time in it. If they found it preposterous, or simply untenable, I had better desist at once from developing it further. I did of course have all the materials I had been meticulously gathering on the use of *keigo*, and this in itself would form a good set of results, so it would not be the end of the world if they poured scorn on my ideas. But it was a nerve-racking exercise. I also had to work on presenting the whole thing in Japanese, which is no mean task to one whose language had been acquired much more in the countryside than in the classrooms of a university.

Takako was still helping me, of course, and she agreed to assist with converting my draft paper into an academic presentation. It was not easy to order, as the ideas were still being gathered and mulled over, but we wrote over half of the paper in a formal style. I continued writing, but the time we had available together ran out, and the language became less formal as I went along. The last section was hurriedly scribbled on the train on the way to Tokyo, in a completely colloquial style, and the paper was then as ready as it would ever be. There were appointments to attend, and there was no further time to fuss.

Although we still had a couple of months of our stay remaining, I took the opportunity of this visit to Tokyo to make enquiries about our return trip. We had a return ticket, via Moscow, and I thought it would be fun to stop off and spend some time there. It was necessary to secure a visa, and since my children had had to have their own passports to travel out to Japan, they had also to have separate visas, at some considerable expense. The exercise of ordering them was interesting, however, for when I went to pick them up, one was filled in incorrectly. The Japanese travel agent who was taking care of the arrangements took it back and promised to send it on when corrected. I might have looked a little concerned about entrusting my son's passport to the post office, but it did arrive safely – wrapped in no fewer than three separate envelopes, each a size larger than the other, fitting together like 'Chinese boxes', or, indeed, Russian dolls. What more care could I seek?

Andrew, my fellow-anthropologist from Oxford, was presenting a paper the day before mine, so I was able to hear how he was developing his ideas about concentric circles, and, in particular, the notion of 'centre'. In the evening Professor Suzuki took the two of us out to a local hostelry, where he ordered the waiter to bring us a taste of all the most delicious food they had available. We spent a very pleasant evening, with Professor Suzuki revealing a definite propensity to seek uniqueness in his personal life, as well as for his country of birth. He keeps a list of the things he doesn't do that others do, he said, and he reeled off quite a number, including drinking, which he was actually engaged in at the moment he said it. 'Well, very little, compared to others,' he qualified, when we laughingly pointed this out to him.

My paper, the following day, was very well attended. In the staff common room, where Professor Yoshida had invited me to take a cup of tea before it started, I met the professor who had helped me with my first research in Kyushu, over ten years previously. He had travelled all day to be there, and I felt very honoured, though a little more nervous. It was good to see him again, however, and we fell to catching up. His research had continued in much the same direction, meticulous and careful, and I wondered how he would feel about my hastily penned piece. I was introduced to one or two other professors who were coming along, among them Professor Miyake, a well-known religious studies specialist who was co-editing a book for Professor Yoshida's retirement, and a self-confident young man who had just returned from taking a sociology PhD at Yale.

My presentation was fairly basic. I noted how impressed I had been with the materials used for wrapping gifts in Japan, and the way that the return gift I received after Tamaru-*san*'s father's funeral had had no fewer than seven layers. I also commented on the way housewives served everything wrapped at their tea parties, and the value which seemed to attach even to the careful wrapping of groceries. I explained the nature of my initial research, summarised the work I had been doing, and began to develop the idea of language as a form of wrapping. I went on to talk of the wrapping of the body, the wrapping of space, and the wrapping of time, as I perceived it, and I gave examples of some of the parallels I had noticed.

It was when I was putting that part of the paper together that I was able to draw in some of the early casual observations I had entered in my diary. The relationship between language and dress worked well, and the comparison between kimono and tennis dress produced smiles of agreement. The pilgrims' trail I had ventured to explore could be interpreted as a way of wrapping space, as could the thin, straw rope tied all around the houses involved in the Yahata Festival. The layout of offices fitted it, as did the organisation of the PTA meeting, which actually proved to have parallels at many a gathering, for business and pleasure.

With slightly less confidence, in the presence of Professor Miyake, I talked about the religious forms of wrapping I had observed, the investigations I had carried out on the language people use when speaking to the gods, and the observations I had made about the unwrapped nature of offerings made to them. Since shrines and temples offer a series of rituals, such as purification through washing or wafting incense, and the removal of shoes as one approaches the most sacred central areas, I proposed that there may be a process of 'unwrapping' which allows greater contact with the sacred.

Even as I was presenting the paper, I realised that the way it moved from formal language, through less formal but carefully written language, to the colloquial scribblings of the train journey was 'unwrapping' the argument in a parallel way, also exemplified by the

PTA meeting. I explained even more informally at the end that all my ideas were at a very early stage of development, and would those present please dispense with polite forms of wrapping their comments, and reveal to me their honest views of what I had said. I had not intended for the paper to 'unwrap' itself in terms of formality, but I didn't let that be known, and the results were quite amazing.

The first comment was devastatingly candid. It was the man who had returned from Yale, and he didn't really like my approach at all, but his criticisms were as unformed as his presentation, and he did little more than confirm that my ideas were still at an early stage. The next day, Professor Yoshida rang me up to tell me to ignore him. It seems he had already run into trouble with Andrew. A linguist who was present did not like the way I considered dialect and *keigo* together, as different forms of wrapping, which Yoshida saw as an inability to stand outside his own system, and Professor Miyake made some deep, detailed comments about the religious ideas which I was at that precise moment unable completely to follow.

Otherwise, the reactions of my audience were largely positive. The anthropology students, who came drinking afterwards, were full of further ideas and suggestions, and they seemed to find the whole framework fun and interesting to discuss. One of a set of twins currently studying with Professor Yoshida, who had previously told me about the levels of politeness they use, launched into a folk classification used by their mother, who lived in the country. If someone gives you a gift of fruit or vegetables, he said, it is usually wrapped in newspaper. If it were not, his mother would say it was 'dirty', using a word, *kitanai*, which she also used to describe certain forms of language. I had heard this word used to describe the Toyama dialect, though not the Kyushu one.

Another student present joined in to point out that if something were handed over unwrapped, it could be commented on as *mukidashi de* (i.e. 'naked', 'bare') *shitsurei* ('rudeness'), in other words, it would be rude not to wrap the object. These comments added to my parallels, and suggested an interesting set of oppositions between words for 'clean' or 'pretty' (*kirei*) and 'dirty', or perhaps 'crude' (*kitanai*), 'polite' or 'careful' (*teinei*) and 'rude' (*shitsurei*), and 'wrapped' or 'covered' and 'unwrapped' or 'naked'. In general, the wrapping principle seemed to be associated with cultural sophistication of one sort or another. The Japanese words indicated this, and it even worked quite well in English.

The students also went on to talk about 'naked relationships' (*hadaka no tsukiai*), which are particularly close, so that the level of wrapping also has a distancing effect, as I had noticed at the Nodas' New Year party. This had a nice parallel with the 'naked speech' I had already been investigating with the boys. The idea also informed the common Japanese expression *enryō shinaide*, which is used to put visitors at their ease. It is often translated as 'don't stand on ceremony', but it literally means 'don't make polite distance'. I had learned, however, that it could be dangerous to take the expression too seriously. Levels of politeness, particularly amongst women, are adjusted to express increasing intimacy, but can be readjusted if one side feels the relationship is becoming too close.

Throughout the evening several people came over to tell me how interesting they had found the ideas, so I felt that the presentation had been a success. I had also gathered some new examples to think about, and I felt justified in continuing the wrapping approach. Later, as I made my way to the house of some friends in another part of Tokyo, I picked up some cakes as a present. It was the only box I could find at the last open shop near the station, but it was wonderfully wrapped. Each cake had a cellophane wrapping, they were arranged in the box with a slip of paper over the top of them, and the box itself was wrapped in gift paper. The salesperson wrapped it all up again, and slipped it into a carrier bag.

As my friends enjoyed the cakes, and their wrapping, I recounted the subject matter of the paper to them. They were also enthusiastic, and came up with several further ideas and examples. We sat up late, but I doubt that it was their hospitality, my cakes or even the earlier drinking that caused the sickness which I suffered during the night and the next day. I was so weak I could hardly drag myself home, and I slept throughout the whole of the following day. It could have been a bug of some sort, but no one else suffered from it. I suspect that the problem was caused by worry, largely suppressed, that the fine tissue of knowledge and understanding that I had been so carefully piecing together would be crushed and destroyed, like an old-fashioned model aeroplane flying into the trees. It wasn't, but it was apparently too late to tell my internal organs about it.

Only a couple of days after I recovered, we received a visit from some old friends from the previous research period, when I had lived near the kindergarten. They were country people whose boys had commuted in by bus, and, as they had been in Hamish's class, we had been invited over to their village on several occasions. During that period, I had rented a car, so it was easier to drive out there, but this time I had only seen them during their local festival when they had come to pick us up. The two mothers, who came with their children, explained that it was difficult for them to get away, since they lived with the senior generation, who were getting old and unwilling to be left on their own.

They spent the morning with us, and then accepted an invitation to lunch, conspicuously making the most of the special circumstances that had allowed them to escape from their usual domestic ties. It was fun to see them again, for we had spent happy times a few years before, visiting the huge greenhouses where they cultivated carnations, and staring in amazement at the sheds where they kept cattle – in a proximity quite shocking to eyes used to seeing such beasts wandering in the fields. Their old, wooden houses were also constructed in an expansive, traditional style, now increasingly difficult to find as recent affluence has brought an abundance of reconstruction and a less interesting architectural standardisation.

The most exciting part of the visit from the point of view of my research, however, was to be found in the abundance of gifts they brought along. There were carnations, stocks and chrysanthemums – enough to fill three large bowls – apples, oranges and strawberries, pots of coffee and instant milk, and a bag of crisps and other snacks for the children. It was not, of course, the abundance which caused the excitement, especially as I anticipated a request for help with their English at the end, but the way in which they were wrapped. The fruit and flowers were carefully packed in newspaper, just as the twins had described, and the coffee and powdered milk were enclosed in a brown paper bag.

They were presents, yes, and the style of presentation was 'clean', but more informal than that usually adopted amongst the townsfolk we had been spending our time with this visit. I listened carefully to the language, and noted that it was polite, but again less formal than that of my more sophisticated housewifely group. It was not really the 'crude', *kitanai*, language of the local dialect, but perhaps an upmarket country version. I remembered the formal greetings we had made, on our knees, when we visited their homes, and the way our visit was confined to the front rooms, leaving the family area at the back unaffected, where the older generation could preserve their privacy.

This visit began to suggest that another version of the wrapping phenomenon, which I had developed during my visit to Kyushu, worked here too, out in the country. That same afternoon, after our guests had left, I went out to return a typewriter I had borrowed from a teacher who lived near the Awa Shrine. Her house was of a modernised country style, and the rest of her family sat 'inside', watching TV, whilst we talked and took tea in the front room. She was quite forthcoming about the use of language in this rural area where she was born, and how it differs from that used in the town where she worked. I made an appointment to carry out a proper interview later. It was one thing to have second-hand ideas from anthropology students, good though they might be, but I could feel properly confident having them confirmed in my own ethnographic notes.

Chapter 21

An artistic farewell

Careful efforts are made to bring the project to a close and ask all outstanding questions, but new ideas don't dry up just because it's time to go home.

The last two months of our visit sped by at an alarming speed. In the early weeks, I had set up various contacts and planned out areas for further investigation. Some of these proved fruitful, others less so, and the major part of our stay was devoted to gathering materials which were likely to contribute to a successful and coherent piece of work. Interviews were planned to cover a range of people as far as possible representative of the different types identified, and it seemed prudent to consult as many 'experts' as possible. Inevitably questions arise in later conversations which can only be answered by returning to earlier ones. That one can follow these up is one of the great advantages of long-term fieldwork, but it all takes time.

As I had learned from previous trips, it is useful to keep a running list of 'questions', because these are best addressed to more than one informant, and they can fill a pause in conversation in all kinds of situations. Towards the end of our stay, I was invited to address the local Rotary Club, for example, and I tried out some of my ideas over lunch. The teachers also asked the local English teacher and me to give a talk, and we were expected to party with them afterwards. It was also quite informative to chat to people on trains, or in shops and restaurants. Foreigners are quite rare, even in this seaside resort, and people are curious enough to open up in exchange for answers to their questions. These conversations can be quite casual as the research progresses, but towards the end one needs to try to ensure that all the gaps are filled.

A bitter-sweet problem which arises towards the end of fieldwork in

Japan is that many of one's new-found friends and acquaintances wish to hold some kind of farewell party. They are aware that these are likely to be numerous, however, and they begin to issue invitations long before the leaving date, which tends to add a sense of urgency to the final round-up of notes and papers. Since cost and distance usually make a return visit prohibitive before one needs to commit the work to print, it is especially important to allow enough time, when planning the last stages, for impromptu interruptions to disturb the final activities, at least in the interest of long-term goodwill.

Many people drop round with gifts, and their numbers must be multiplied by the number of people in the house. Whilst I could leave Jenny, who was anyway staying on a little after we left, to take care of her own affairs, I felt obliged properly to thank people who brought presents for the children. It is also a good idea to keep a very careful record of who has brought what, for a Japanese person returning from a trip will bring appropriate gifts for all those who gave them leaving presents. I had found things escalating a little too far when I first went back to Kyushu, however. The trip took place a couple of years after Hamish was born, and I had to procure two enormous extra bags to carry home all the toys and other gifts I received in return for my returns.

It is also very important, if one plans to go back, to keep very clear records of people's names, addresses, occupations and relations amongst themselves. Because of the unusual nature of the visit of an anthropologist, the people we meet are likely to remember us better than we will them, and those who seemed so very familiar during the period of fieldwork will remain in one's mind as a face, possibly with lots of shared experience, but vital details may slip away. In the case of Kyushu, my notes of who lives where and what they do are the first thing I pack when returning, and I can now chat to adults who were children when I first went about grandparents they hardly remember. It was important to have this material clearly recorded before I left Toyama too.

In practice, we tidied up quite nicely. Arranging for a shipment of luggage helped, for we could dispose of the abundance of papers and objects we had collected in advance of our departure, and several people were thoughtful enough to bring their farewell gifts in time to catch this consignment. Callum's baseball team gave him a very good send-off, contributing to an enormous personal team flag for him to take home, and a brand new uniform to replace the borrowed one we had agreed to return. Hamish had acquired a large number of small, 'cute' objects from his 6th year girlfriends, which needed careful packing, and his classmates had put together a wonderful album of photographic memories.

The school headmaster and his wife took the three of us for a very splendid day out a couple of weeks before we left. They ascertained which local sights we had not yet seen, and took us on a tour in their car. It was a little difficult to relax with a man who commanded such a distant position within the school, but I think the boys enjoyed themselves, and it was a good opportunity for me to tie up some of our previous conversations. Our departure fell at the end of the academic year in Japan, and the school graduation ceremony had been an interesting formal experience we could discuss. Few fail to move on to middle school, but this says little about their ability, he admitted. The formal progress from year to year is taken for granted, and the teachers must do their best by each child.

A fairly formal farewell party was organised by the tea teacher, who engaged the help of my classmates to cook a splendid meal. These were the same people who had gathered at New Year, and they presented me with a very pretty lacquer-ware tea container, carefully packed in a box, which was enclosed in gift paper signed with all their names. I had taken along some chocolates for the occasion, quite an unusual gift in Japan (outside Valentine's Day), and these were opened and shared out amongst those present. The wrapping paper was carefully torn into sections large enough for each to contain and carry the requisite number home. As the time came to leave, we engaged in a series of deep bows, exchanging words of thanks, with the teacher noting the difficulties associated with parting.

There were several other farewells, augmented by the fact that Takako and her family were moving to a different part of Japan, after living in Toyama for several years. The end of the school year, which also happens to be the financial year, is a good time to move if moves have to be made, and there was an atmosphere of change in the air. We were invited to a very pleasant dinner at the 'eel shop', hosted by the Hosaka hospital family, primarily for Takako's family, but it was nice to be included. The tennis group also arranged a party at a special hotel following our last meeting, and they presented me with smart watches for myself and each of the boys.

Paradoxically, perhaps, the most interesting visit in the last few days was to the house of some people we had never met before. This was at the invitation of the shakuhachi player, who rang to see if I'd like to join him on a visit he had to make to a famous artist who lived in the area. Evidently the artist had sent a gift to the koto player who had

Figure 8 A 'farewell ceremony' at school for the anthropologist's sons before they leave Japan

shared his concert in Tokyo, and he was taking along a return gift. Pressed for time, I certainly hesitated before agreeing to make a new contact at this late stage, but Ishii-*san* was most persuasive, and it would be our last chance to meet him too, it seemed. In the event, it was well worth the few hours it took.

He picked me up in the car, with his wife and 2-year-old son, so it was quite a family outing. The drive was not too long, though our destination was a few miles from the town, but we parked at some distance from the house we were to visit. It was then necessary to continue on foot, down a narrow lane through a bamboo grove, eventually to arrive at a beautiful house and garden quite hidden from the road. The architecture was of a modern Japanese style, though with some interesting idiosyncrasies, such as long windows, instead of the latticed paper *shōji*, opening onto the veranda, which was itself constructed to overhang a large lake at one side and a garden at the other. Inside, there was much space, and very little clutter.

The effect was marred somewhat by the desperate efforts of the occupants to control a barking dog, unusually living inside the house, for it is more often the custom in Japan to keep dogs in kennels outside. This was no ordinary couple, however, as one could see immediately. They were wearing loose corduroy suits, identically fashioned in a subdued sandy colour to fit both male and female forms. Both also had their heads completely bald, although it looked as if, whilst the artist himself had simply lost his hair, his wife had shaved her head in sympathy.

Their house was full of treasures, hanging scrolls, paintings and pots, although they were not all immediately on display. Indeed, I was able to witness the wonderful anticipation of having a dusty box brought out to the table, to be gradually and gravely unpacked. There were invariably inner layers to be peeled off, and Ishii-*san* whispered that the number and quality of these were indications of the value of the object inside. He told me later that the artist had clearly thought me worthy of considerable respect, for he had opened one of his most prized possessions, a pot from the Kamakura period (twelfth–fourteenth centuries). Apparently such valuable items lose something in the opening process, so he only rarely gave this one an airing.

I was unqualified to appreciate the artistic merit of the pot itself, despite the artist's confidence, but it was extremely valuable for me to learn that the wrapped state has such importance. To keep things out on display is actually to demean them, in a Japanese view, it seems, and to dispose of their boxes and other wrapping materials is quite literally to deprive them of their worth. It is on the box that the name of the artist and his (or her) stamp is engraved, and without this proof a pot can become almost worthless. It was also an interesting idea that the choice of materials to show to a visitor could indicate his or her status, but it was of course parallel to choosing appropriate language, and selecting appropriate clothes to wear.

The artist gave me some tickets to an exhibition of his work then taking place in Nara, unfortunately too far away for a visit at this stage. He also presented me with a copy of a limited edition of a book of poetry, illustrated by his ink paintings, with an original watercolour on the front that Ishii-*san* later estimated to be worth some 200,000 yen. That was between £800 and £1,000 at the time, but I have never tried to test his estimate. Money was clearly no problem in this house, for the artist then produced a painting for the koto player which was executed on material made for him by a paper-maker who had achieved the status of 'national living treasure'. Its value, per sheet, was apparently some 10,000 yen, that is, between £40 and £50.

The Ishiis' small son was becoming restless by this time, and his continual racing around was growing alarming. Eventually he tripped off the veranda into a puddle in the garden, and this was deemed the moment to leave. All the way home, Ishii-*san* sang the praises of the artist, which is just as well, for my own aesthetic sense had not really been well enough tuned to pick up his evident excellence. Still, the visit had been enlightening, and it opened up a couple of new lines of thought which would keep me on my toes after my return.

In fact the 'wrapping phenomenon' kept me occupied for several years after we got back to the UK. There were plenty of loose ends to be tied up, and as many new ones emerged as I went around talking about my ideas in anthropology departments here and elsewhere. I had also gathered publishable material about the use of speech levels, and sharing activities with Takako's group had given me some excellent insights into the secrets of the housewifely arts. As a parent of children in a primary school, with an especially cooperative set of teachers, I had picked up some valuable inside knowledge about how the achievements of Japanese children depend on more than the content of the curriculum.

All in all, it had been a very productive visit, and as we boarded the train to make our way back to the airport, we gazed sadly out at the town we had now twice made our home. The headmaster waved us off at the station, as did some other friends, but this time Takako was with us, moving on to her own new life. She solemnly wrote her new address out for me before we reached the station where we would alight. We didn't have too much to say on this occasion. We were both tired from the frantic last-minute activities. For both of us, it was the end of an era, and although we, personally, would spend a few brief visits together, our children would be in their mid-teens before they would meet again.

Afterword

If you have enjoyed reading this account of life in the field for an anthropologist, you may like to follow it up with an example of field-work in another part of the world, with a different initial research plan. The following list includes some of the better known works of this kind, and also illustrates a change in approach of the writers concerned, through time, as the importance of revealing personal feelings about the experience gradually came to be realised in the wider anthropological community. Initially it had seemed unscientific to introduce too much of the observer, and there was considerable controversy about whether Malinowski's (1967) diary should be published at all. Smith Bowen is a pseudonym chosen by an anthropologist who published an albeit somewhat fictionalised account of her fieldwork experience in 1954, and other anthropologists, such as Nigel Barley (1983), David Maybury-Lewis (1965) and Brian Moeran (1985), chose a different writing style to distinguish their personal accounts from the ethnographies which became their more 'official' contributions to the academy.

The works of Rabinow (1977), Dumont (1978) and Cesara (1982) began to raise serious questions about the influence of the personality and gender of the fieldworker on the outcome of the research, however, and their contributions coincided with the beginning of a debate which questioned the whole validity of research carried out in a way which was so dependent on the personal experiences and writing style of the fieldworker (see, for example, Clifford and Marcus 1986; Geertz 1988). The edited volume by Okely and Calloway (1992) both defended the method and argued for the importance of making explicit autobiographical details of both the researcher and their principal informants, and their book includes a selection of examples. It has now become almost expected that some detail about the personal circumstances of the author will be included in any ethnography, so that the reader can incorporate this information into his or her understanding of the people being described.

I hope that this present volume has illustrated the advantages of the personal involvement of a fieldworker in gaining an understanding of a society which is based on deeply held assumptions quite different from that of the observer, and at the same time the need for this kind of research for making clear the existence of such differences in an increasingly open and homogenised cosmopolitan world.

Further reading

Barley, N. (1983) *The Innocent Anthropologist: Notes from a Mud Hut*. London: Penguin Books.

Berreman, G.D. (1972) Behind Many Masks: Ethnography and Impression Management. In G.D. Berreman, *Hindus of the Himalayas. Ethnography and Change*. Berkeley: University of California Press.

Cesara, M. (1982) *Reflections of a Woman Anthropologist: No Place to Hide*. London: Academic Press.

Clifford, J. and G.E. Marcus (eds) (1986) *Writing Culture: The Poetics and Politics of Ethnography*. Berkeley: University of California Press.

Dumont, J.-P. (1978) *The Headman and I: Ambiguity and Ambivalence in the Fieldwork Experience*. Austin, TX: University of Texas Press.

Gardner, K. (1991) *Songs from the River's Edge*. London: Virago.

Geertz, C. (1988) *Works and Lives: The Anthropologist as Author*. Cambridge: Polity Press.

Huxley, F. (1956) *Affable Savages*. London: Hart-Davis.

Lévi-Strauss, C. (1955) *Tristes Tropiques*. Paris: Plon; translated into English, first as *World on the Wane* (1961) London: Hutchinson, and then under the orginal title (1973) London: Jonathan Cape.

Malinowski, B. (1967) A *Diary in the Strict Sense of the Term*. London: Routledge.

Maybury-Lewis, D. (1965) *The Savage and the Innocent*. London: Evans Brothers.

Moeran, B. (1985) *Okubo Diary*. Stanford: Stanford University Press.

Okely, J. and H. Calloway (eds) (1992) *Anthropology and Autobiography*. London: Routledge.

Rabinow, P. (1977) *Reflections on Fieldwork in Morocco*. Berkeley: University of California Press

Rosaldo, R. (1993) *Culture and Truth: The Remaking of Social Analysis*. London: Routledge.

Smith Bowen, E. (1954) *Return to Laughter*. London: Victor Gollancz.

Spindler, G.D. (1970) *Being an Anthropologist: Fieldwork in 11 Cultures*. New York: Holt, Rinehart and Winston.

Index

housekeeping 53–4, 107
housewives(') xii, 6, 19, 40, 53–5,
    114, 121, 143; group 30–2, 53,
    104–5, 146, 153 *see also nakama*;
    'professional' 19, 54, 58, 60; skills
    54, 135
husbands 55, 104, 106–7, 111, 136–7

ideas 144–5, 148, 153
identity 37, 48, 64
ideology ix, 136
idiosyncracy 103, 129, 151
ikebana 32, 85–9; Ikenobo school of
    89; Sōgetsu school of 89
illegality 15
image 72, 79, 92, 137
immigration procedure 26
impoliteness 6
Inbeshi 38
incense 68, 70, 143
indirect communication 95–6
individuality 132
informality 31, 57, 88, 90, 103,
    110–11, 125, 127, 144, 146
informant 18, 69, 72, 92, 110, 131,
    148, 154
information viii, 139–40
inside and outside space 85, 146–7
insider 125
insight viii, 4, 52, 54, 67, 72–3, 75,
    83, 91, 153
inspiration 4, 135
insult 84
intent(ion) 95;122
international: communication 94;
    language 94; press 98
interpretation viii
interview(s) ix, 28, 39, 53, 57, 62, 65,
    75, 77–9, 102, 110, 114, 124, 129,
    133, 147, 148
intimacy ix, 15, 31, 62, 125, 145;
    levels of 104
investment 123, 125
invitations 94, 121, 125, 131, 137,
    145–6, 148–50
irony 104
Ise Shrine 114

Ishii family 135–6; Masumi 136; Mrs.
    113, 135; Tōzan 111–13, 150–3
isolation 115
Izuki, Mr. 14–15, 101

Japan Alps 121
Japan Socialist Party 79
Japanese: lifestyle 9; mafia, *see
    yakuza*; nationality 64; naval
    defence forces 68; occupation of
    Korea; point of view 96; school
    system xiii, 63; society 69, 92
Jenny, see Davidson
journeys 92

Kabuki 31, 37
kadomatsu 122
kamaeru 47
Kamakura period 152
kana 75
kanji see Chinese script
Kannon deity 38
karaoke 39
karmic destiny 35
kata 31
Kawana family 17
kawatta 13
keigo 5, 14, 18–20, 27, 40, 57–8, 93,
    96, 105, 110, 141; used in
    ceremony 112, 124; level of 88;
    used in meetings 131; variety of
    xi-xiii, 62, 129; as wrapping 115,
    144
Keio University xiv, 91, 94, 141;
    Institute of Language and Culture
    96, 141
kimono 72, 83, 87, 89–90, 103, 138,
    143
Kinkonkan 92–3, 106
kindergarten 5, 7, 26, 30, 54, 56–8,
    131, 133, 139, 145; funds 58
kirei 144
kitanai 144, 146
kneeling 89, 126, 146
knowledge viii, 4, 132, 134, 136, 139,
    145; differential dissemination of
    72; esoteric 103; gulf in 83; inside
    153

university 20, 42, 91, 94, 139; degrees 137
unwrapping 115–16, 141, 143–4, 152
upbringing 19, 136

Valentine's Day 132–4, 150
violence 40–1
visa 25, 64, 142
volcanic: display 101; dust 100, 102; eruption 99, 102–3
volcano 98–102; and evacuation of people 99, 100, 102

Wakayama prefecture 123
waste of resources 72
wealth 93
weddings 27–8, 72, 113
Western: art 112, 131; attire 48; body 9; dishes 106; fairy tale 106; flower-arrangement 87; flute 112; food 92, 113; model 107; origin 31; research ix; room 9; sewing 32; standards 107; table setting 109, visitor 135
white 93; gloves 93; paper 49, 74, 88; uniform 68
White Day 133
White Lily Kindergarten 4, 6, 14, 56–8, 60, 62, 103–5, 110, 113, 129, 139; Bazaar 58, 103–4, 131, 136
wishes 123

women('s): group 13; managers 75–9; university 94
words: fixed 71
work 19; mates 121; place 5, 91
working women 55, 135–6
World Cup 62
worship 33, 115
wrapping xi, xii, 67, 70–4, 84, 111, 129–30, 145; bodily 138, 143; as communication 72; 'corners' 93; of feelings 115; of food 58, 113–14; forms of 91, 93, 144; groceries 143; ideas 141, 144; level of 145; paper 25, 70, 93, 125, 150; people 72, 88, 130, 136; phenomenon 117, 125, 146, 153; principle 144; scheme 113, 116; of space 75, 78, 85, 88, 109, 143; special 124; of time 130–1, 143; types of 135; value of 152; verbal 72

yakuza 40–2, 46–7, 65–6, 122, 137–40
Yale University 143–4
Yamada, Mrs. 63–5
Yamanote 19, 47, 130
Yoko, *see* Hirose
Yorkshire pudding 105–6
Yoshida Teigo xiv, 141–4
youth 46–7, 133, 134

Zen Buddhism 112, *see also* Ishii